THE HOURS OF HENRY VIII

THE HOURS OF HENRY VIII

A Renaissance Masterpiece by Jean Poyet

ROGER S. WIECK

WILLIAM M. VOELKLE

K. MICHELLE HEARNE

GEORGE BRAZILLER · PUBLISHER
in association with
THE PIERPONT MORGAN LIBRARY

New York

François Avril and Myra Orth kindly shared their wise opinions
on manuscripts they knew much better than I. Will Noel played good buddy.
And Jean-François made it all possible.—R.S.W.

First published by George Braziller, Inc., in the United States of America in 2000

Text and images copyright © 2000 by The Pierpont Morgan Library

For information, please address the publisher:
George Braziller, Inc.
171 Madison Avenue
New York, NY 10016

Library of Congress Cataloging-in-Publication Data

Wieck, Roger S.
    The hours of Henry VIII : a Renaissance masterpiece by Jean Poyet / Roger
S. Wieck, William M. Voelkle, K. Michelle Hearne.—1st ed.
        p. cm.
    Illustrations previously attributed to Jean Bourdichon are currently attributed
to Jean Poyet.
    Includes bibliographical references.
    ISBN 0-8076-1477-7
    1. Hours of Henry VIII—Illustrations. 2. Books of hours—France—
Illustrations. 3. Poyet, Jean, fl. 1465–1503. 4. Bourdichon, Jean, 1457?–1521? 5.
Illumination of books and manuscripts, French. 6. Illumination of books and man-
uscripts, Renaissance—France. 7. Pierpont Morgan Library. I. Voelkle, William M.
II. Hearne, K. Michelle. III. Poyet, Jean, fl. 1465–1503. IV. Bourdichon, Jean,
1457?–1521? V. Title.
ND3363.H57 W54 2000
745.6'7'092—dc21   00-039758

Frontispiece: Self-portrait of Jean Poyet as St. Luke Painting the Virgin, from the
"Briçonnet Hours"; Haarlem, Teylers Museum, MS 78, fol. 8v, detail (see pp.
20–23). The miniatures from the "Hours of Henry VIII" are reproduced at
approximately 107%.

Photography of the "Hours of Henry VIII" by Joseph Zehavi
Design by Rita Lascaro
Printed and bound in China

FIRST EDITION

Dedicated to John Plummer

who taught us about Jean Poyet

CONTENTS

FOREWORD

The Hours of Henry VIII, unlike the Library's previous publications on medieval and Renaissance manuscript illumination, represents a notable departure: it is the Library's first monograph devoted to the oeuvre of a single illuminator. It is published upon the occasion of the Library's first ever one-man show devoted to an illuminator, "Jean Poyet: Artist to the Court of Renaissance France." Until recently, Jean Poyet, who was in his own day even more famous than his well-known rival, Jean Bourdichon, had been all but forgotten. Both of these Renaissance illuminators worked in Tours for the French court, where they painted manuscripts for, among others, the bibliophile queen of France, Anne de Bretagne. Poyet, unfortunately, had a relatively short career, and his acclaimed masterpiece— the subject of the present monograph—was later even attributed to his rival. The aim of this book is thus to reexamine, restore, and bring to greater public attention the reputation that Poyet enjoyed during his own lifetime. That the book should be dedicated to John Plummer is highly appropriate, and I would like to add my voice to those of the authors in acknowledging the fundamental role he played in their own studies.

Although John Pierpont Morgan had already acquired two important manuscripts illuminated by Poyet—the tiny, but exquisite Prayer Book of Anne de Bretagne and the Lallemant Missal—it was the acquisition of the Hours of Henry VIII that made the Library preeminent as a repository of Poyet's works, and thus a logical institution to generate both the publication and exhibition. The manuscript, however, was not a purchase, but the gift of the Heineman Foundation for Research, Educational, Charitable, and Scientific Purposes. Dannie H. Heineman had the foresight to purchase the book as a gift for his wife (Belle da Costa Greene, the Morgan Library's first director, had twice refused to buy it). Hettie Heineman subsequently bequeathed it to the Heineman Foundation. We are therefore extremely grateful to the late James H. Heineman and the Trustees of the Heineman Foundation for their magnificent gift, in 1977, of the Heineman Collection, and for establishing and augmenting an acquisitions endowment that continues to support the growth of the collection. Although the Hours of Henry VIII could not have been made for that king (his putative ownership descends from an eighteenth-century tradition), it did belong to a series of later English monarchs, including George III. The stature of the manuscript as Poyet's uncontested masterpiece makes the gift all the more important. It is thus appropriate that the monograph, for the first time, should reproduce all of its miniatures in color, making it possible for everyone to share and enjoy Poyet's supreme achievement.

Generous support for the Poyet project was provided by Michel David-Weill; the H. P. Kraus Fund for Lectures, Research, and Acquisitions in Medieval and Renaissance Manuscripts; James E. Ferrell; Bruce Ferrini; and the Andrew W. Mellon Research and Publications Fund. Additional assistance was received from the Marilyn M. Simpson Charitable Trust and the Samuel H. Kress Foundation. Hank Walter contributed special media support. Our thanks, too, to lenders to the exhibition: the collection of Frances Beatty Adler and Allen Adler, New York; an American private collection; the Art Institute of Chicago; the Bibliothèque Nationale de France, Paris; the British Library and British Museum, London; the Free Library of Philadelphia; the Museum Boijmans Van Beuningen, Rotterdam; Mrs. Alexandre Rosenberg, New York; the Teylers Museum, Haarlem; and the Walters Art Gallery, Baltimore.

Finally, I would like to add special thanks to my colleagues Roger Wieck, who supervised the publication of this beautiful facsimile and organized the exhibition, and William Voelkle and Michelle Hearne, his co-authors.

Charles E. Pierce, Jr.
Director
The Pierpont Morgan Library

INTRODUCTION

The Hours of Henry VIII is a splendid manuscript. It receives its name after a tradition—which is possible but thus far unproved—that holds that King Henry VIII of England once owned the book (see the discussion of provenance in appendix B). In any case, Henry would not have been the manuscript's original patron. The book was created around 1500 when Henry, born in 1491, was only nine years old; the manuscript was clearly made for an adult (it contains, for example, none of the prayers for children found in pedagogical Books of Hours made for young eyes). Secondly, the manuscript was not made for English use, and any Book of Hours written for Henry would have been made for English (that is, Sarum) use and would have contained English saints in the Calendar, Litany, and Suffrages. Who originally commissioned the book is not, and will probably never be, known, as the manuscript contains no marks of ownership—no names, obituaries, coats of arms, mottoes, or portraits. But what we do know about this luxurious book—that its miniatures are of the highest quality and can be attributed to the artist Jean Poyet—is enough to warrant their reproduction in color in this publication. As the pages from the Hours of Henry VIII reveal, Poyet was a master colorist and a genius at composition and perspective.

The study that follows is divided into three main sections. Chapter 1 discusses the position held by the Hours of Henry VIII within the history of Books of Hours. In chapter 2 the oeuvre of Jean Poyet is described, including the place of the Hours within this body of work. These chapters are followed by the suite of color reproductions, accompanied by commentary, of all the miniatures (and two of their facing text pages) from the Hours of Henry VIII. Appendices offer a physical description of the manuscript (including a collation diagram), the history of its provenance, and bibliographies (including one keyed to a list of Poyet's principal works).

As discussed in the second chapter, Poyet's reputation in the nineteenth century was quite high. He was thought to have painted the miniatures and flowers in the *Grandes Heures* of Anne de Bretagne, the most popular and famous illuminated manuscript in the nineteenth century. (The subscribers to the grand full-color chromolithographic facsimile—the first ever of its kind—published in 1841 included Emperor Napoléon III, Pope Pius IX, and Emperor Alexander II of Russia.) This attribution to Poyet was a complete mistake, however, and when a payment document linking Jean Bourdichon to the *Grandes Heures* was published in 1880, Poyet's fame began to fall. Attached to a fabulous manuscript and to a famous queen, the name of Jean Bourdichon immediately rose high and bright in the art historical firmament. Soon, any manuscript of any quality illuminated in the Touraine in the late fifteenth or early sixteenth century was given to Bourdichon or his workshop (including the Hours of Henry VIII). By the earlier part of the twentieth century, Poyet was pretty much forgotten.

Poyet's Lazarus-like resurrection took place in 1982. In his exhibition at the Morgan Library, "The Last Flowering: French Painting in Manuscripts, 1420–1530," and in the accompanying catalogue, John Plummer attributed a body of high-quality work—distinctive for its palette and perspective—to Jean Poyet, the only contemporaneous rival of Bourdichon. Eleven years later, François Avril and Nicole Reynaud in their 1993 Bibliothèque Nationale exhibition catalogue, *Les manuscrits à peintures en France, 1440–1520,* expanded Poyet's oeuvre and further defined his style. In 1999, the Morgan Library's charming little Prayer Book of Anne de Bretagne, which Poyet illuminated for that queen of France and the dauphin, was published in a complete facsimile accompanied by a lengthy commentary. The present volume, which contains the fullest treatment to date on the artist, publishes what is considered Poyet's masterpiece, the Hours of Henry VIII. And, finally, in 2001, again at the Morgan Library, the artist will be fêted with a one-man show, the first ever presented by the Library for an illuminator.

CHAPTER I

The Hours of Henry VIII as a Book of Hours

For three hundred years, from the mid-thirteenth to the mid-sixteenth century, the Book of Hours was *the* bestseller of the late Middle Ages and the Renaissance. From 1250 to 1550, more Books of Hours were specially commissioned firsthand, bought and sold secondhand, and passed down from mother to daughter and from father to son than any other book, including the Bible. And by the late fifteenth century, when printing made the Book of Hours cheaper and thus available to a whole new category of customers, nearly any literate soul could buy one.

There are a number of reasons behind this immense popularity. The first is the book's contents. The Book of Hours is a prayer book that contains, as its heart, the Little Office of the Blessed Virgin Mary, that is, the Hours of the Virgin. (For this reason, the Latin term for the book is *Horae,* which means "Hours.") The Hours of the Virgin are a sequence of prayers to the Mother of God that, ideally, were recited throughout the course of the entire day, sanctifying it through her to God, Hour by Hour. The Book of Hours played a key role in the late medieval and Renaissance cult of the Virgin. Marian devotion placed the Mother of God in the pivotal role as intercessor between humankind and God. As our spiritual mother, Mary would hear our petitions and take mercy on our plight. She would plead our case to her Son, who, surely, could not deny his own mother anything for which she asked. In a Europe dominated by cathedrals dedicated to Notre Dame, the Hours of the Virgin were deemed Our Lady's favorite prayers, the quickest way to her heart. Other prayers in *Horae* helped round out the spiritual needs of late medieval and Renaissance men and women. The Penitential Psalms, for example, were recited to help one resist temptation to commit any of the Seven Deadly Sins. The Office of the Dead was prayed to reduce the time spent by one's friends and relatives in the fires of purgatory.

Another reason Books of Hours were so popular was because of the people who used them: the laity. In a kind of bibliophilic jealousy, laypeople during this period sought for themselves a book that paralleled the use and function of the Breviary, the book containing the Divine Office, from which the clergy prayed daily, and the

3

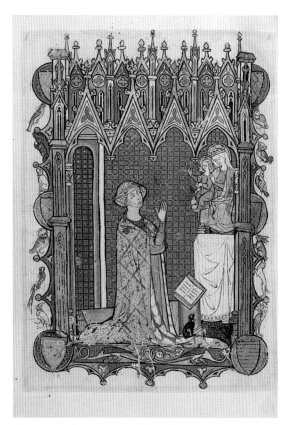 

Fig. 1. A Lady (Contesse de la Table?) of the Coeuvres Family at Prayer, from the "Psalter-Hours of Yolande de Soissons"; France, Amiens, 1280s–90s. New York, Pierpont Morgan Library, MS M.729, fol. 232v.

Fig. 2. Virgin and Child Adored by Hawisia DuBois and Her Family, from the "DuBois Hours"; England, London, c. 1325–30. New York, Pierpont Morgan Library, MS M.700, fol. 3v.

Missal, used by the priest at Mass. In an age when rood screens in churches blocked all but the most fleeting views of the Mass, when squints were pierced into chapel walls in an effort to offer some glimpse of the Elevation of the Eucharist, when, in other words, the laity's access to God was very much controlled and limited by others, Books of Hours bestowed direct, democratic, and potentially uninterrupted access to God, the Virgin Mary, and the saints.

In fact, this period represents the first time since classical antiquity that a genre of book was in the hands, not of a select few (that is, the ordained of the Catholic Church), but of a sizable portion of the general population. At this time, the lay population of Europe was both more literate and wealthier than those of the early and high Middle Ages. This smarter, richer population seized upon the Book of Hours as *the* household book. If a family owned but one book, it was thus going to be a Book of Hours. While a *Horae*'s main use was obviously for personal prayer, it could also help keep track of time (all Books of Hours contained Calendars), serve as a family archive for genealogical records (birth, death, and marriage notices were often inscribed onto flyleaves), and assist in teaching children to read (ABCs and such basic

4

prayers as the Our Father and Hail Mary appear in special *Horae* made for young eyes). Furthermore, a Book of Hours was a not so subtle way of showing off one's wealth: illumination was expensive, and one paid for each and every picture, gilt initial, and colored line-filler. Finally, owners of Books of Hours used coats of arms and portraits of themselves and their families to boast of or promote their social standing.

The illumination, especially the pictures, also contributed much to the continual popularity and success of Books of Hours. As well liked now through reproduction on Christmas cards as they were then in their original context, such pictures were often the only form of art owned by a middle-class family. Even to the wealthy, who could commission paintings and tapestries for their castles or chapel walls, miniatures in Books of Hours were a continuous source of aesthetic pleasure. One did not need more than one Book of Hours, but those who could afford to sometimes owned several; Jean, duc de Berry, owned about fifteen.

Horae linked church and home. The subjects illustrated in a typical Book of Hours—the Infancy and Passion of Christ, miracles and martyrdoms of the saints— were the same as those painted onto altarpieces or stained into glass in a church.

Fig. 3. Master of Sir John Fastolf, William Porter Adoring the Virgin and Child, from the "Hours of William Porter"; France, Rouen, c. 1420–25. New York, Pierpont Morgan Library, MS M.105, fols. 84v–85.

Fig. 4. Master of the Gold Scrolls, St. Christopher Carrying Christ, from a Book of Hours; Belgium, Bruges, 1440s. New York, Pierpont Morgan Library, MS W.3, fol. 167v.

Books of Hours, which could be used at home or at church, linked chamber with chapel. An example printed in 1538 in Rouen for export to England by Nicholas le Roux for François Regnault contains a preamble, "The Preface and the Manner to Live Well," whose instructions (spelling modernized) reveal how a Book of Hours was actually used:

First rise up at six of the clock in the morning in all seasons and in your rising do as follows. Thank Our Lord of rest that he gave you that night, commend you to God, Blessed Lady Saint Mary, and to that saint which is feasted that day. . . . When you have arrayed yourself in your chamber or lodging, [say] Matins, Prime, and Hours if you may. Then go to the church . . . , and abide in the church the space of a low mass, while there you shall think and thank God for his benefits. . . . When you are come from the church, take heed to your household or occupation till dinner time. . . . Then take your refection or meal reasonably, without excess or over much. . . . Rest you after dinner an hour or half an hour as you think best. . . . As touching your service, say unto Terce before dinner, and make an end of all before supper. And when you may, say Dirige [Office of the Dead] and Commendations for all Christian souls, at the least way on the Holy Days and, if you have leisure, say them on other days, at the least with three lessons. . . . (PML 19585, fols. C6r–C8r)

The Hours of Henry VIII was produced at a very interesting moment within the history of Books of Hours. In their first two hundred years (mid-thirteenth to mid-fifteenth century), illuminated Books of Hours were for the most part luxury items. They were expensive and produced largely on demand. In other words, they were special commissions and not manuscripts that a bookseller would, or could, afford to keep stocked on his shelves. Examples from the Morgan Library's own collection include the stellar thirteenth-century Psalter-Hours commissioned by a lady (possibly Comtesse de la Table) of the Coeuvres family (fig. 1); the imposing *Horae* that Hawisia DuBois had made for herself and her family in the fourteenth century (fig. 2); and the fat and voluminously illustrated Book of Hours with which the

Englishman William Porter rewarded himself for his helpful part in the capture of Rouen in 1419 (fig. 3).

In the second quarter of the fifteenth century, however, the marketing of Books of Hours began to change. In the 1440s, booksellers in Bruges began to sell large numbers of Books of Hours illustrated with inserted pictures. Because they were inserted (and with no text on their backs), these pictures, often painted by the Flemish illuminators collectively known today as the Masters of the Gold Scrolls, could be as few—or as many—as one could afford. Thus the Book of Hours as an affordable commodity came to be. With limited means, for example, one might buy only an Annunciation, Penitent David, and Burial, to mark the three most important texts, the Hours of the Virgin, Penitential Psalms, and Office of the Dead. With more money to spend, one might add a miniature of the Four Evangelists for the Gospel Lessons, a complete suite of eight pictures for the Hours of the Virgin, and a sprinkling of images illustrating the Suffrages (fig. 4).

Just a generation later, in the 1460s and '70s, Willem Vrelant (fl. 1449–81), working in Bruges, and Maître François (fl. c. 1460–80), in Paris, used another method to get illuminated Books of Hours into the hands of even more people (figs. 5, 6). They

Fig. 5. Workshop of Willem Vrelant, Flight into Egypt, from a Book of Hours; Belgium, Bruges, c. 1470. New York, Pierpont Morgan Library, MS M.30, fol. 114v.

Fig. 6. Maître François, Coronation of the Virgin, from a Book of Hours; France, Paris, c. 1470. New York, Pierpont Morgan Library, MS M.73, fol. 66.

standardized and streamlined the production process. Each master produced a set of workshop models (which would be varied slightly) for the customary dozen or so pictures of a typical Book of Hours, and then each artist hired a large number of assistants whose essential talent was not originality but the ability to paint like his boss.

Such routine *Horae* were clearly the bread and butter of these artistic entrepreneurs; while assistants cranked out the Books of Hours, the masters themselves had more time for the special—more interesting, challenging, and better paid—commissions.

By the mid-1480s in Paris, another development took place that was significant not only for the *Horae* market, but also for the book trade in general. Until then, early printers were producing books largely for the same class of people who could afford expensive manuscripts. Now Parisian printers found that they could also make money by selling cheaper books to a larger market. Using print, paper, and woodcuts, they created illustrated Books of Hours that cost a lot less to produce than those written by hand, executed on vellum, and illuminated with suites of unique paintings. Produced cheaply, the printed *Horae* could be sold for much less than their manuscript counterparts (fig. 7). They could be—and were—bought by many more, and

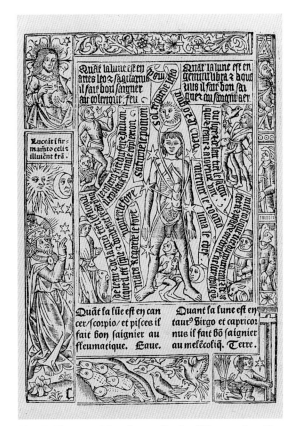

Fig. 7. Planetary Man, from a Book of Hours printed by Philippe Pigouchet for Enguilbert, Jean, and Geoffroy de Marnef; France, Paris, c. 1488–91 (almanac 1488–1508). New York, Pierpont Morgan Library, PML 127562 (ChL 1475X), fol. a2v.

much less well off, people. And this new group was clearly delighted with its purchases! Many of them had probably never owned a book before. Thus the first mass-market book was born. Between 1480 and 1600 there were some 1,775 different *editions* of the Book of Hours printed in Europe.

Competition between illuminators and printers created a red-hot market. Like a Ping-Pong game, influences shot back and forth rapidly between the two media. Imitating fancy manuscripts, printers began to add more and more scenes to their historiated borders (fig. 8); illuminators retaliated by hiring hacks to crank out amusing border vignettes. Printers upgraded the appearance of their product by using metalcuts, which offered finer, more detailed images; illuminators fought back by stealing their iconography. From the late fifteenth to the first quarter of the sixteenth century, the production of both manuscript and printed Books of Hours peaked. This acceleration in both camps, geared to the lower end of the market, resulted in the creation of thousands of books and manuscripts that were visually appealing but, it must readily be admitted, not always of the highest quality.

Taste (and human snobbery) being what it is, there will always be people who, whether by birth or income, feel the need to rise above what they see as the common (pun intended) denominator. In other words, while Books of Hours were falling into the hands of more and more people, there remained, at the very, *very* high end of the market, a demand for luxury items. While these included deluxe printed editions, hand-colored and executed on vellum, expensively illuminated manuscripts were specially commissioned. Those with money—and the desire to show it off—especially sought out the unique piece created by *the* artist of the moment. The Hours of Henry VIII is just such a book. With its large size, many pictures, and seamless execution by Jean Poyet, one of the French court's favored artists, it ranks with the finest French Books of Hours of its period.

Poyet is one of a small group of illuminators whose elegant style appealed to the richest and most powerful men and

Fig. 8. Flight into Egypt, from a Book of Hours printed by Antoine Chappiel for Gillet Hardouyn; France, Paris, 24 November 1503. New York, Pierpont Morgan Library, PML 19286, fol. E3v.

women of France. He worked for the courts of three successive French kings: Louis XI, Charles VIII, and Louis XII. One of his great patrons was Anne de Bretagne, twice queen of France (wife of Charles VIII and of his successor, Louis XII). From Poyet she commissioned a fancy prayer book to teach her firstborn, the dauphin Charles-Orland, his catechism (New York, Pierpont Morgan Library, MS M.50); a small Book of Hours for which, importantly, the payment document survives (the only extant leaf from this manuscript might be in Philadelphia; Free Library, Lewis E M11:15a); and an abbreviated Psalter, painted in grisaille, that Anne apparently used while between husbands (Paris, Bibliothèque Nationale de France, MS lat. 2844). These and other manuscripts by Poyet are discussed and illustrated in the following chapter.

Fig. 9. Jean Bourdichon, Pentecost and Lentil Flowers, from a Book of Hours; France, Tours, c. 1515. New York, Pierpont Morgan Library, MS M.732, fols. 29v–30.

Poyet had only two peers: Jean Bourdichon (1457–1521) and an anonymous artist known as the Master of Anne de Bretagne (fl. c. 1480–c. 1510). Of all his French contemporaries, only these two could compete with Poyet in terms of quality and style. A native of Tours like Poyet, Bourdichon, too, was patronized by the court. His most famous manuscript—famous, especially, for the hundreds of accurately rendered flowers in its borders—is the *Grandes Heures* painted for Anne de Bretagne before 1508 (Paris, Bibliothèque Nationale de France, MS lat. 9474). A Book of Hours in the Morgan Library, painted by Bourdichon a few years after he finished the *Grandes Heures,* also features botanically correct flowers in its borders (MS M.732; fig. 9). The Master of Anne de Bretagne, who worked in Paris, is named after the *Très Petites Heures* he illuminated for the French queen, who, the reader will by now have gathered, played a major role in commissioning first-rate manuscripts from France's top illuminators (Paris, Bibliothèque Nationale de France, MS n. a. lat. 3120). The Morgan Library's Hours of Anne of Austria, named after Louis XIII's queen, who owned the book in the seventeenth century (MS M.1110; fig. 10), was painted around the same time—about 1498—as Anne de Bretagne's *Très Petites*

Fig. 10. Master of Anne de Bretagne, Annunciation, from the "Hours of Anne of Austria"; France, Paris, late 1490s. New York, Pierpont Morgan Library, MS M.1110, fol. 37.

Fig. 11. Simon Bening, Mass of the Five Wounds of Our Lord, from the "Da Costa Hours"; Belgium, Bruges, c. 1515. New York, Pierpont Morgan Library, MS M.399, fol. 36v.

Heures. The Anne de Bretagne Master was a busy man, for in addition to illumination, he had his hand in designing images for printed books (the metalcuts, for example, of the exquisite Book of Hours printed by Philippe Pigouchet on 22 August 1498), stained glass (the rose window for Sainte-Chapelle in Paris), and tapestry (the Hunt of the Unicorn series in the Cloisters Collection of the Metropolitan Museum of Art in New York). He was so busy that, in a way, he was not real competition for Poyet; in fact, compared to his output in other media, his illuminations are pretty scarce. Bourdichon, on the other hand, was Poyet's rival. He was designated official court painter by Louis XI in 1481, a status he maintained, through successive kings, to Francis I. He also had the advantage of longevity over Poyet: Bourdichon lived till 1521, whereas Poyet was dead by 1503. To judge by the numerous royal commissions dating from the first two decades of the sixteenth century, Bourdichon, aided by his tireless shop, was only too happy to fill the void left by Poyet's death.

France, of course, was not the only country where there flourished a sizable niche market for specialty manuscripts in the age of print, as the following exam-

Fig. 12. Master of Charles V, Emperor Charles V in Prayer, from the "Hours of Charles V"; Belgium, Brussels, c. 1540. New York, Pierpont Morgan Library, MS M.696, fol. 56.

Fig. 13. Giulio Clovio, Baptism of Christ, from the "Farnese Hours"; Italy, Rome, 1546. New York, Pierpont Morgan Library, MS M.69, fol. 35.

ples from the Morgan Library reveal. In Flanders, for example, fine Books of Hours were illuminated by Simon Bening (1483/84–1561), whose fans were from not only Belgium but also Italy, Germany, and Portugal. Bening's great Da Costa Hours was originally made for a member of the Portuguese Sá family, from whom it passed to King Manuel's armorer, Alvaro da Costa (fig. 11). Discriminating collectors kept up the demand for unique, hand-painted Flemish Books of Hours till the middle of the sixteenth century. Emperor Charles V, for instance, had fine taste in illumination; tradition holds that he took a Flemish Book of Hours with him when he retired to the monastery of Yuste, in Spain (fig. 12). In Italy, shortly after it was completed, the Book of Hours that Cardinal Alessandro Farnese commissioned from Giulio Clovio (1498–1578) was already regarded as the most famous manuscript of the High Renaissance; according to Vasari, Clovio labored nine years on the work (fig. 13). And, returning to France, Claude Gouffier, whose important governmental posts included First Gentleman of the Privy Chamber and Master of the Horse of France, commissioned a Book of Hours grandly painted in the Mannerist style (fig. 14), the text of which, ironically, was copied from a printed *Horae.*

Textually, the Hours of Henry VIII comprises a number of prayers and devotions that were in vogue in France at the cusp of the late Middle Ages and Renaissance (for an outline of the book's texts, see appendix A). The manuscript opens—indeed, as does every *Horae*—with a Calendar. Next come the customary four Gospel Lessons, one by each evangelist, followed by the Passion according to John. John's passage, narrating the events of Christ's Passion (which had not been covered by the traditional four readings), became, by the late fifteenth century, a standard fifth Gospel Lesson. Following these five

Fig. 14. Master of the Gouffier Hours, Coronation of the Virgin, from the "Hours of Claude Gouffier"; France, Paris, c. 1550–58. New York, Pierpont Morgan Library, MS M.538, fol. 47v.

biblical excerpts appears a suite of four Marian devotions. First are the two popular prayers to the Virgin that were often paired: the *"Obsecro te"* and the *"O intemerata";* these are followed by the *"Stabat mater."* A major theme of all three of these prayers is the fidelity of Christ's mother during his Crucifixion (the *"Stabat mater,"* of course, remains popular today). The fourth Marian devotion is the Mass of the Virgin. Next come the Hours of the Virgin—the heart of any Book of Hours—followed (as was typical in late French *Horae*) by the Hours of the Cross and the Hours of the Holy Spirit. After these are the Penitential Psalms (with the Litany), the Office of the Dead, and the popular Seven Prayers of St. Gregory. Next is a long series of twenty-three Suffrages; these petitions to individual saints are arranged in the medieval hierarchical sequence in which the male saints come first, female saints second (the whole series, however, begins with an unusual Suffrage to St. Jerome preceding the one to the Trinity, which is normally the first). The book ends with a group of practical prayers that were increasingly popular in the late fifteenth and early sixteenth centuries. These prayers (as their rubrics tell us) were to be said upon waking up, when leaving the house, upon entering a church, before a crucifix, and at the

Elevations of the Mass. These prayers are unillustrated (as is normally the case) and are thus often ignored by the art historian, but this is unfortunate since their presence and sequence tell us, for example, about the everyday religious practices and pietistic concerns of the user of the manuscript. These prayers are also evidence of the fact, mentioned above, that Books of Hours were used both at home and at church. The sequence ends with the Athanasian Creed; different from the Apostles' Creed, which medieval and Renaissance Catholics were expected to have memorized as children, the Athanasian Creed makes frequent appearance in late Books of Hours (it played the role of a canticle in Breviaries and was recited daily at Prime by the Church's ordained).

While pictorially rich, the Hours of Henry VIII is not iconographically innovative. The subjects of the miniatures are, for the most part, not unusual and can be found in many a French Book of Hours from the period. (The elaborate historiated borders that accompany forty-one of the miniatures are the book's most unusual feature.) What is innovative and unusual about the manuscript is its style. Jean Poyet's art has fluidly merged the cool late Gothic aesthetic of his native, northern France with the avant-garde Renaissance style of northern Italy. Like Jean Fouquet (c. 1415/20–c. 1481) shortly before him and Nicolas Poussin (1594–1665) many years later, Poyet successfully married North with South. The next chapter will discuss Poyet's oeuvre and the place, within it, of the Hours of Henry VIII.

CHAPTER II

The Artist Jean Poyet and His Oeuvre

Although the attribution of the Hours of Henry VIII to Jean Poyet has gained wide acceptance, the artist's oeuvre is not without its vexing questions. The chief components of this body of work, the attributions to it, and the issues surrounding it will be examined here.*

Documentary Sources

Relatively little is actually known about the historical person of Jean Poyet. He is presumably related in some way (as a son?) to a Mathelin (or Maturin) Poyet, a Tours artist who was paid eight *livres* five *sols tournois* in 1453 for painting a shield with the arms of the king. A 1465 document mentions a Jehan Pohier who is paid eight *livres* five *sols* and, in a second entry from the same year, thirty-five *sols* for painting various heraldic work. Is this our Jean Poyet? It seems likely. As we shall see, by 1483 Poyet was already a mature artist executing major commissions and having already traveled to Italy; he could easily have been born around 1445, which would have made him about twenty years old in 1465 when he could have executed the heraldic work.

The first mention universally agreed upon to be the artist we call Jean Poyet appears in documents of April 1483 when he is paid more than 157 *livres tournois* for a total of 1,031 coats of arms that he painted to be attached to the candles and torches used at the funeral for Queen Charlotte of Savoy, wife of Louis XI (it was quite common in this period for artists to do what we today might consider pedestrian work). The same 1483 document lists, a little later, a *"Jehan Poyet, paintre,"* among those who received black cloth to make a mourning robe and *chaperon* (hood) to wear at the funeral. The fact that Poyet is listed with others from her retinue implies that the painter had an official position at Queen Charlotte's court. Poyet received three measures *(aunes)* of cloth, a reflection of his good position (valets received two *aunes,* while the highest ranking officers got three and a half).

The second time Poyet's name appears (spelled "Poyer" and, in a part of the document not quoted below, "Poiet"), it is among the names of other local Tours artists

---

*An earlier and shorter version of this chapter appeared in my publication *The Prayer Book of Anne de Bretagne.*

who were paid for work on decorations celebrating the ceremonial entry into Tours by Anne de Bretagne as queen of Charles VIII on 23 December 1491. The document is worth quoting from because it reveals how Poyet was apparently the impresario of the event—at least of the mystery plays *("misteres")*—designing, making, organizing, and orchestrating the spectacles. The document also reveals how hard he worked—day and night—during the festivities and how his efforts were appreciated:

> *Item, audit Jehan Poyer, qui aussi à Henry Lallement, peintres, la somme de XLII l[ivres].; c'est assavoir la somme de XVI l[ivres]. t[ournois]. qui leur fut promis pour leurs peines et sallaires d'avoir vacque durant le jeudi, vendredi, sabmedi et dimanche, jour et nuyt, a faire, diviser, ordonner et conduire tous lesdits misteres cydessus declerez, et la somme de XXXVI l[ivres]. t[ournois]. pour les rembourser de plusieurs autres parties qu'ilz ont fournyes de leur mestier à faire lesditz misteres, oultre et pardessus les autres choses cydessus declerées, dont pour ce a esté composé au dict Jehan Poyer; pour ce, XLII l[ivres].*

> *Item, to the said Jehan Poyet, as well as to Henry Lallement, painters, the sum of 42 livres; that is to say, the sum of 16 livres tournois, which was promised to them for their work and salaries for having spent during Thursday, Friday, Saturday and Sunday, day and night, in producing, designing, planning and managing all the said mysteries described above, and the sum of 36 livres tournois for them to reimburse many other parties who had furnished them with their expertise to make the said mysteries, over and beyond the other things described above, which were made by the said Jehan Poyer; for the work, 42 livres.*

The third mention of Poyet occurs in an entry for 29 August 1497 in Queen Anne's accounts. There Poyet (called *"enlumineur et historieur, demourant audict Tours"*) was paid a little over 153 *livres tournois* for illuminating a *"petites heures"* for the use of Rome that Anne had commissioned (the scribe Jean Riveron was also paid 14 *livres* for writing the book and securing its vellum). For this small Book of Hours, Poyet provided twenty-three miniatures *("histoires riches")*, 271 borders *("vignetes")*, and 1,500 line endings *("verses")*:

> *A Jehan Riveron, escripvain demourant à Tours, pour avoir escript, à la main, unes petites heures, que ladicte dame a faict faire, à l'usaige de Romme, et pour avoir fourny de velin. . . . XIIIJ liv[res].*
> *A Jehan Poyet, enlumineur et historieur, demourant audict Tours, la somme de sept vingt treize livres trois sols tournoys, pour avoir faict ès dites heures, vingt trois histoires riches, deux cens soixante et unze vignetes, et quinze cens verses; par marché faict, avec lui, par ladicte Dame, laquelle somme de VIIˣˣXIIJ l[ivres]. IIJ s[ols]. IIIJ d[eniers]. luy*

a este payée, baillée et délivrée comptant, par ce présent trésorier, par vertu desdits roolle
et mandement, dont est faicte mention, ainsi qu'il appert par sa quitance, cy rendue, dat-
tée le XXIX jour de aoust, l'an mil CCCC quatre vings et XVIJ, montant semblable
somme de VII^{xx}XIIJ l[ivres]. IIJ s[ols]. III d[eniers]. t[ournoys]. pour ce icy ladicte
somme de VII^{xx}XIIJ l[ivres]. III s[ols]. III d[eniers]. t[ournoys].

To Jehan Riveron, scribe living in Tours, for having written, by hand, a small Book
of Hours, which the said lady [Anne de Bretagne] *had commissioned, for the use of*
Rome, and for having furnished the vellum. . . . 14 livres.

To Jehan Poyet, decorator and illuminator, living in the said Tours, the sum of 153
livres 3 sols tournois, for having made in the said Book of Hours, 23 rich miniatures,
271 borders, and 1,500 line endings; as per the contract between him and the said lady,
that is, the sum of 153 livres 3 sols 4 deniers, which has been paid, presented, and deliv-
ered promptly to him by the present treasurer, by virtue of the said role and authority,
which is mentioned here so that it appears in this receipt, dated the 29th day of August,
the year 1497, totaling the sum of 153 livres 3 sols 3 deniers tournois, for the said sum
of 153 livres 3 sols 3 deniers tournois.

The fourth and final time Poyet's name can be found in documents is in 1498. On 12 September the town fathers of Tours met to discuss the decorations for the royal entry of Louis XII. Assigned to supervise the play reenacting Petrarch's *Triumphs* was Poyet (spelled here "Pohier"). Poyet had had a similar job in connection with the entertainments for Anne's entry in 1491.

Literary Sources

In addition to the documents cited, Poyet's name occurs in three sixteenth-century printed books. The context in all three is revealing. In *La Plaincte du Désiré* (Lyons, 1509), written by Jean Lemaire de Belges on the occasion of the death of Louis de Luxembourg in 1503 (the poet later became part of Anne de Bretagne's court), the talents of Poyet are equated with those of Rogier van der Weyden (1399/1400–1464) and Hugo van der Goes (c. 1440–1482) in a song of praise that also singles out the illustrious company of Simon Marmion (c. 1425–1489), Jean Fouquet, and Jan van Eyck (c. 1395–1441):

> *Et si ie n'ay Parrhase ou Appelles,*
> *Dont le nom bruit par mémoires anciennes,*
> *I'ay des esprits recents & nouvelets,*
> *Plus ennoblis par leurs beaux pincelets*
> *Que Marmion iadis de Valenciennes,*
> *Ou que Foucquet qui tant eut gloires siennes;*

Ne que Poyer, Roger, Hugues de Gand,
Ou Ioannes qui tant fut élégant.

And if there is no longer Parrhasius or Apelles,
Whose names resound through ancient memories,
There are recent and new geniuses,
More ennobled by their fine touch,
Such as [Simon] Marmion once of Valenciennes,
Or [Jean] Fouquet who was himself so famous,
Or [Jean] Poyer, Roger [van der Weyden], Hugo van der Goes,
Or Jan [van Eyck] whose art was so refined.

Jean Pélerin (known as Viator) cites Poyet in his *De artificiali perspectiva* (Toul, 1509; second edition), the first printed book on perspective with illustrations and one of the outstanding Renaissance texts on the subject (along with Leon Battista Alberti's *Delle pittura libri tre* of 1435–36, and Albrecht Dürer's *Unterweysung der Messung*, Nuremberg, 1525). The poem on the title-page lists Poyet just after Fouquet:

O Bons amis, trespassez et vivens,
Grans esperiz, Zeusins, Apelliens
Decorans France, Almaigne et Italie,
Geffelin, Paoul, et Martin de Pavye,
Berthelemi Fouquet, Poyet, Copin,
André Montaigne et d'Amyens Colin . . .
Plus précieux vous tiens que telz joyaux,
Et touz autres nobles entendemens
Ordinateurs de specieux figmens.

O good friends, dead and living,
The great geniuses, Zeuxis and Apelles,
Deem you who embellish France, Germany, and Italy,
[Olivier] Geffellin, Paoul [Goybault], and Martin of Pavia,
Bartholomew [van Eyck], [Jean] Fouquet, [Jean] Poyet, Coppin [Delft],
Andrea Mantegna and Colin d'Amiens . . .
More precious than any jewel
Or any other nobly talented
Creator of special art.

And, finally, half a century later, Poyet's skills in perspective and painting were rated above those of Fouquet and his two sons by Jean Brèche of Tours in *De verborum significatione* (Lyons, 1556):

Scatet enim celebris haec ipsa nostra Turo omni artificum excellentissimorum genere. Inter statuarios et plastas extitit Michael Columbus, homo nostras, et qui coelebs totam vitam egit, quo certe alter non fuit praestantior. Inter pictores Joannes Foucquettus, atque ejusdem filii Lodoicus et Franciscus. Quorum temporibus fuit et Joannes Poyettus, Foucquettiis ipsis longe sublimior optices et picturae scientia.

Indeed this our city of Tours itself has given birth to a race skilled in the most excellent of the arts. Among sculptors and carvers our Michel Colombe is prominent; he remained unmarried his entire life and was certainly surpassed by no other. Among painters there were Jean Fouquet, as well as his sons Louis and Francis. And in the same period there was Jean Poyet, even more gifted than the Fouquets in perspective and the art of painting.

The documentary sources, though spartan, can tell us much about Jean Poyet. They reveal that he was living and working in Tours from at least 1483 (or probably 1465) until at least 1498. They describe an artist whose work was sought out by three royal courts, those of Queen Charlotte, Queen Anne de Bretagne, and King Louis XII. At least at one of these courts—Queen Charlotte's—he had an official position. We learn that Poyet, like many artists of his time, painted the mundane (coats of arms for candles) and the magnificent (the *"petites heures"* for Queen Anne herself). He was an able organizer, a good manager, and a hard worker. An assignment by the city of Tours to stage Petrarch's *Triumphs* indicates that he was most likely not only literate but also intelligent enough to deal with foreign source material. This picture of a bright career is further burnished by the literary sources. They compare Poyet's abilities with those of such internationally famous artists as Jean Fouquet and Simon Marmion from France; Rogier van der Weyden and Hugo van der Goes from Flanders; Lucas van Leyden (c. 1494–1533) and Hans Baldung Grien (1484/85–1545) from Germany; and Leonardo da Vinci (1452–1519) and Michelangelo Buonarroti (1475–1564) from Italy. The combined documentary and literary sources, in other words, conjure up a great artist with a fine and appreciated career.

Rise, Fall, and Restoration of Poyet's Reputation

In the nineteenth century, the 1497 payment document for the *"petites heures"* was linked to that period's favorite illuminated manuscript, the *Grandes Heures* of Anne de Bretagne (Paris, Bibliothèque Nationale de France, MS lat. 9474). The fact that the document's tally of decoration (miniatures, borders, and line endings) did not match those found in the *Grandes Heures* did not keep authors from insisting that the 1497 payment was indeed for Anne's *Grandes Heures* and that therefore Jean Poyet was the artist of this most fabulous of manuscripts. Poyet's reputation was so well regarded that even after the payment document linking Jean Bourdichon to

Anne's *Grandes Heures* was published in 1880, some writers still insisted on Poyet's participation, assigning him its famous flowers, and giving Bourdichon the miniatures. This forced notion did not last long. Like a wilted bloom, Poyet's name was largely discarded in the early part of the twentieth century and, when the *"petites heures"* of the 1497 document could not be located, his career took a nosedive and he was pretty much forgotten. Any illumination of any quality (and much that was not) was now generously attributed to Bourdichon (including the Hours of Henry VIII).

More recently, in the 1980s and '90s, Poyet's career has made a comeback. A body of work, roughly contemporaneous with that of Bourdichon (and which had often been attributed to him), was seen as different. Two major exhibitions—"The Last Flowering" in New York in 1982 and *"Quand la peinture était dans les livres"* in Paris in 1993—established an oeuvre for Poyet. In 1999 a facsimile, with lengthy commentary, of the charming Prayer Book of Anne de Bretagne (Pierpont Morgan Library, MS M.50), which the artist illuminated for that queen of France, was published. Poyet's oeuvre, however, is not without controversy. As Janet Backhouse in the new Grove *Dictionary of Art* points out, the evidence for all attributions to Poyet, while seductively convincing, remains circumstantial since there is not a single surviving documented work. Analyzing the context of the names in the literary sources cited above, one scholar recently argued that the historical Poyet must have been dead by 1503 since his name is lauded among a group of artists who were all dead by that date. Because more than one art historian has attributed to Poyet work dated well into the second decade of the sixteenth century, this argument logically calls into question the wisdom of applying Poyet's name to the body of work now associated with it. Thus two, not unrelated, questions about Poyet and the historical record remain. First, are there any surviving works that can be linked with the payment documents to Poyet? And, second, does Poyet's putative death around 1503 destroy the oeuvre? Because I offer a "maybe" to the first question and definite "no" to the second, I will maintain that the historical Poyet is—largely, but not completely—the artist of the body of work presently associated with him. The reasons behind my answers to the two questions will be presented in their proper places within the chronological survey of the more important art attributed to Poyet that follows.

Briçonnet Hours

The earliest manuscript that can be given to Poyet is the magnificent Book of Hours in Haarlem (Teylers Museum, MS 78). It can be most likely dated between 1483 and 1491 for reasons of style and, as we shall see, provenance. Because nothing prior survives, we shall consider it part of Poyet's "early" work, although in both style and iconography, it is clearly the creation of an established master. Stylistically, the

Haarlem Hours already exhibits the main characteristics of Poyet's art: a masterful command of clearly articulated space (interiors and landscapes), a frequent accompanying use of chiaroscuro, solid but articulated figures (often in contrapposto), daring color juxtapositions, and a fondness for Italian Renaissance architectural detail. In the David in Prayer (for the Penitential Psalms) many of these features are in evidence (fig. 15). Thick and heavy (in this case) drapery complements the weight, posture, and age of the slightly stooped king. David kneels at an angle to the picture plane, a position emphasizing the figure's three-dimensionality. Behind him, railings establish a clear set of spatial progressions that are further articulated by the buildings on either side of the river. Constrained and directed in the foreground and middle ground, space is then allowed free rein when it spills onto the distant hills. Color in the miniature seems traditional for late fifteenth-century France until one studies the buildings, which are painted in a series of bluish grays, light greens, and lilacs. They are extraordinary shades. In the miniature of St. Matthew (fol. 10), a small angel leans over to whisper in the evangelist's ear: in the small area of their tête-à-tête, Poyet, against a dominant royal blue and red,

Fig. 15. Jean Poyet, David in Prayer, from the "Briçonnet Hours"; France, Tours, 1483–91. Haarlem, Teylers Museum, MS 78, fol. 70.

introduces, among the clothing, a lilac that fades to white and a yellow that turns to orange. The engaging glances exchanged between Matthew and his muse, with their somber flesh tones, white beard, and brown hair, keep the kaleidoscope from spinning out of control. Chiaroscuro, as in other miniatures like the Luke Painting the Virgin (fol. 8v) and the Annunciation (fol. 21), helps define an interior space articulated with Italian Renaissance architectural details.

In the miniature of Mark (fol. 11v), Poyet reveals—boasts of, even—of the source for much of his style: Italy. While the evangelist, accompanied by a husky lion, examines the tip of his quill in the foreground, behind him, through the classical arches of a Renaissance portico, lies Venice. On a canal a gondolier plies the waves over which wood bridges arch. Poyet is letting us know that he has seen the fabled city whose streets are filled with water, the city of which Mark is patron and his lion its symbol. A firsthand knowledge of north Italian art at an early stage of Poyet's artistic development—that is, sometime before the Haarlem Hours—left an indelible impression on the painter and was a continual influence on his work. From his Italian experience—which must have included seeing the early works of Andrea Mantegna (1430/31–1506) and Giovanni Bellini (c. 1431/36–1516)—Poyet borrowed the quiet and pensive dignity of his figures and the stillness and depth of his landscapes. Direct contact with the real thing gave the artist the ability to represent believably Italian Renaissance spaces: Poyet could not have depicted his convincing proportions and idiomatically correct architectural vocabulary had he learned them secondhand.

Iconographically, the Haarlem manuscript is not a typical Book of Hours. Four of its major text divisions are marked not by single pictures but by majestic pairs of images: John's Passion is introduced by miniatures of Joab Killing Abner (or Amasa) and a Betrayal (fols. 12v–13); the Hours of the Virgin by Gideon with the Golden Fleece and an Annunciation (fols. 20v–21); the Penitential Psalms by David Anointed by Samuel and a David in Prayer (fols. 69v–70); and the Office of the Dead by Job on the Dungheap and the Raising of Lazarus (fols. 82v–83). The subjects of the murder by Joab and of Gideon with the Fleece are rare in Books of Hours. They come from such typological handbooks—popular in the fifteenth century—as the *Biblia pauperum* or the *Speculum humanae salvationis*. Even rarer in the Haarlem Hours, however, is the use of the Annunciation of the Death of the Virgin (fol. 60) to mark Compline of the Hours of the Virgin.

While at least one previous author has commented on the charm of the trompe-l'oeil jewels painted within many of the small initials throughout the manuscript (and even attributed them to the Master of the della Rovere Missals), overlooked until now is a small coat of arms tucked within the initial C that begins the text of Matthew's Gospel Lesson (fol. 10v). These are the arms—*azur, bande componée or et gueles de cinq pièces, une étoile or en chef* (blue, diagonal band checkered with five squares of gold and red, a gold star at top)—of the famous Briçonnet family of Tours (as Philippe Palasi has kindly informed me). A likely candidate for the family member who might have commissioned the book is Guillaume Briçonnet, historically known as the Cardinal of Saint-Malo. Before taking the cloth (after the loss of his wife in 1491) and pursuing a successful state-ecclesiastic career, Guillaume had been a family man, married to Raoulette de Beaune and the father of three sons. He was superintendent of finance for Languedoc under Louis XI, who recommended Guillaume to his son and successor on his deathbed in 1483. The young Charles VIII took his father's advice: he appointed Guillaume Briçonnet as France's secretary of the treasury and raised him to first place in the Council of State.

The Briçonnet Hours (as the Haarlem manuscript should now be called) is just the sort of showy gift a man whose stock had risen meteorically might confer on a

Fig. 16. Jean Poyet, *Christ Carrying the Cross, Crucifixion, and Entombment,* from the Passion Triptych; France, Tours, 1485. Loches, Château (photo: Jean-Baptiste Darrasse, Tours).

productive wife. The period of Guillaume's ascendancy from local to national fame, that is, from his promotion in 1483 to the death of his wife in 1491, corresponds with the date span traditionally given to the manuscript (that is, 1485–90). Interestingly, some of the images of the Virgin in the book seem to refer to a real person: in three of the miniatures (fols. 8v [see frontispiece], 40, 54v) the Virgin's hair beneath her veil is coiffed in a fifteenth-century roll, and in a fourth picture (fol. 109) she wears curls! Are these Virgins portraits of Guillaume's wife? Another interesting feature of the book is the miniature of the Holy Family (fol. 112v; it illustrates a series of prayers to the Virgin). Unusual in itself, it is doubly so because of the prominence given to Joseph. Is this image of domestic bliss a reference to Guillaume's happy family? Whichever member of the Briçonnet family did commission the manuscript, he or she cleverly decided upon an artist who was both a local star in the family's hometown of Tours and who was also fashionably in demand at court.

Loches Altarpiece

The second early work by Poyet is the large altarpiece at the château of Loches (near Tours). In triptych form (although its "wings" cannot be shut), the panel contains three scenes: *Christ Carrying the Cross, the Crucifixion, and the Entombment* (fig. 16). It is dated 1485 (M·CCCC·LXXX·V) at the bottom of the left scene, and, in the right scene, "F·I·B" is inscribed near a kneeling monk who wears the white robes of a Carthusian. He is presumably the donor; the initials are thought to refer to Frater Johannes Berandi (Jean Béraud or Béreau), who in 1483 had become prior at the Charterhouse of Liget, which, located in the forests of Loches, was the original home of the triptych. Previously attributed to "school of Fouquet," the work is now regarded as Poyet's only surviving panel. Stylistically, the altarpiece is consistent with the Briçonnet Hours: note the quiet deep landscapes, monumental figures who move believably in space, and daring color juxtapositions. The facial types of the soldiers and the older bearded men, especially Nicodemus and Joseph of Arimathea in the Entombment, are those of which Poyet is so fond. The heroic bodies of the three crucified figures bear witness to Poyet's contact with Italian art.

A commission from the Charterhouse of Liget for a large altarpiece from a major artist like Poyet should not surprise us. Although a tiny town, Loches not only was a short distance from Tours but also had a royal château, one of the many castles owned and visited by King Charles VIII and his queen, Anne de Bretagne. Loches, too, must have held a special place in Anne's heart: around 1500 a chapel at the castle was built for her, its limestone walls marvelously carved overall with her emblems, *cordelières* and ermine tails.

Prayer Book of Anne de Bretagne

The year 1490 begins the decade to which most of Poyet's work can be dated. We will discuss the Prayer Book of Anne de Bretagne first because it can be dated between 10 October 1492 and 6 December 1495, the birth and death dates of the dauphin, Charles-Orland. (The manuscript was probably created toward the end of this period, around 1494–95.) The Prayer Book was commissioned by Anne so she could teach the dauphin his prayers; it is he who is portrayed on folio 31, projected to about the age of twelve. But the style of the Prayer Book is different from that of the Briçonnet Hours and the Loches triptych. Forms and surfaces that had been fixed and hard in these two early works are treated, in comparison, almost impressionistically in the Prayer Book. The careful (and, for the most part, concealed) brushstrokes of the earlier work are replaced here with small, quick applications that are now visible. We can almost feel the artist at work. The edges of things (be they people, fabric, or objects) are ever so slightly blurred, suggesting a slightly hazy atmosphere. Surfaces are alive with tiny jabs of paint. Another significant difference between the early work and the Prayer Book is the palette: in general, it is much lighter. Pastels now dominate. Daring color juxtapositions, which characterize Poyet's early creations, are taken in a new direction. They are now much subtler. Take, for example, the angels holding aloft the Eucharistic monstrance on folio 11v (fig. 17). The robes of the two angels in front are pale lilac, whereas their wings are a light blue; the other two angels are dressed in pistachio green with light purple wings. When a truly solid and intense color appears in the manuscript, such as the dragon's blood in folio 20v, it is almost a shock. This new lightness of tone is paralleled, too, in the Prayer Book in the way the figures are depicted. They now seem lighter, physically so, and move with an easier grace than do the figures in the early work. Proportionately, too, they have changed: taller and more slender, and with smaller heads. Their drapery has none of the thickness and weight seen in the Briçonnet Hours.

In the pamphlet that the Parisian dealer Théophile Belin published to promote the Prayer Book of Anne de Bretagne (prior to its purchase by Pierpont Morgan), a connection is made between the manuscript and a document of 1492. The document records a payment, dating sometime between January and May of that year, for a piece of black velvet for the binding of a book called a *"Patenostre"* (*"pour faire une couverte pour couvrir ung des livres de lad. dame [Anne], nomme le livre de la Patenostre"*). Since Anne's manuscript opens with the words, *"Pater noster,"* the author of Belin's booklet saw it as the volume for which the black velvet was bought. The fact that the manuscript is now bound in red velvet was not deemed a problem (and, indeed, the manuscript is slightly trimmed, indicating that the present red velvet is not the original binding). There are two problems, however, with this proposal. First, Anne's first child, Charles-Orland, was not born until 10 October 1492. It thus seems unlikely that Anne would have commissioned her Prayer Book prior to the actual birth of her child, whose sex, of course, she did not know. (Belin's author, who did not realize the pedagogical function of the manuscript, misidentified the portrait on fol. 31 as Charles VIII.) The second problem with the theory is that it is unclear exactly what type of book a *"Patenostre"* actually is. For example, another document from the queen's accounts from the same year cites a payment for the making of a *"chaisne de patenostres a jour,"* which is clearly a rosary. The *"Patenostre"* manuscript referred to in the 1492 document is thus probably a kind of written

Fig. 17. Jean Poyet, Angels Displaying the Eucharist in a Monstrance, from the "Prayer Book of Anne de Bretagne"; France, Tours, 1492–95. New York, Pierpont Morgan Library, MS M.50, fol. 11v.

rosary, a series of Our Fathers followed by a group of Hail Marys. Such written rosaries, though rare, do exist. A Parisian Book of Hours from around 1500 currently owned by Ursus Rare Books in New York contains three slightly different rosaries, in each of which (amazingly) all the Our Fathers and Hail Marys are completely written out. (The manuscript, once part of the Horace von Landau collection, was sold in London at Sotheby's, 12 July 1948, lot 61.) In this light, it seems prudent to suppose that the *"Patenostre"* book of the 1492 document refers to another (now lost) manuscript and *not* the Prayer Book of Anne de Bretagne.

Fig. 18. Jean Poyet, Annunciation to the Shepherds, from the "Hours of Mary of England"; France, Tours, c. 1495–1500. Lyons, Bibliothèque Municipale, MS 1558, fol. 33v.

Hours of Mary of England

A little larger in size but similar in style to the Prayer Book is the Hours of Mary of England (Lyons, Bibliothèque Municipale, MS 1558); it was probably created a little later, between 1495 and 1500. Poyet painted this manuscript with the light palette and "quick" manner that characterize the execution of the Prayer Book. And if the compositions in the Prayer Book are sometimes simple and the space restricted (for, we must remember, the miniatures were painted with the eyes of a child partly in mind), those of the Hours of Mary of England are more complex. The arrangement of the folios is also more elaborate, with each miniature set into a Renaissance frame that extends into the bottom border and is painted to look like the frame's sturdy architectural base (fig. 18). Further embellishment is added by the frolicking putti who play with garlands in front of many of these bases.

Lacking any coats of arms or mottoes, the manuscript does not reveal its original owner. It does, however, have an interesting later history. Sometime in the second decade of the sixteenth century the book was slightly remodeled. A bifolio was added (between the Calendar and the Gospel Lessons) with a Suffrage to St. Jerome illustrated with two miniatures: Jerome in Penance and a Landscape with a Donkey and Lion. The two pictures are not by Poyet but by the Master of Claude de France, an artist (named after illuminations he created for Anne's daughter Claude) who was active only in the second decade of the century. A leaf was also added (between the Passion according to John and the Hours of the Virgin) with a Suffrage to the Blessed Sacrament illustrated by a miniature of Two Angels Holding a Host and a Chalice; this picture is by Jean Bourdichon (Poyet's rival in Tours). Inscriptions within the manuscript indicate that it had been given by Louis XII after the death of Anne de Bretagne, the king's second wife, to Mary Tudor of England, his third wife. The manuscript had apparently been picked up by Louis secondhand as a ready gift for his new wife. This marriage, which lasted but a few months before Louis died, was in 1514. Returning to England after the quick death of her spouse, Mary then gave the book, again as an inscription tells us, to her brother the king, Henry VIII. The fact that the later remodeling, which must have been around the time the manuscript became a bridal gift, was executed by artists other than Poyet might be significant. It might lend support to the theory, discussed below, that by the second decade of the sixteenth century, Poyet was no longer around.

Single Leaf of the Lamentation

Quite close in size and style to the Prayer Book of Anne de Bretagne is a single leaf in the Free Library of Philadelphia with a miniature that can be attributed to Poyet (Lewis E M11:15a). This previously unpublished leaf is small (3⅞₆ x 2³⁄₁₆ in., that is, 8.7 x 5.5 cm) and comes from a Book of Hours. The text on the recto of the leaf is the conclusion of Mark's Gospel Lesson: *". . . [mor]tiferum quid biberint, non eis nocebit . . . sequentibus signis"* (Mark 16:14–20), followed by the invocation, *"Deo gratias. Per evangelica dicta deleantur nostra delicta."* The text is framed by a thin gold line, and the margins contain a generous sprinkling of the letter *E* (fig. 19). In blank space below the Gospel text a French inscription has been added. On the verso is a miniature of the Lamentation (fig. 20). At the bottom of the picture's simple architectural frame are written the opening words of the prayer, *"Obsecro te domina."* In French Books of Hours of the late Middle Ages, the *"Obsecro te"* (often followed by the other favorite prayer to the Virgin, the *"O intemerata"*) typically follows the Gospel Lessons.

The most important of the previously discussed Poyet documents records the 1497 payment for the twenty-three miniatures, 271 borders, and 1,500 line endings that the artist painted in a small Book of Hours for Anne de Bretagne. This manuscript is not known to have survived. But could the Philadelphia leaf be a folio from this long-lost book? There are persuasive reasons to believe so. Although today in distractingly bad condition, the Lamentation is by Poyet himself (the figure of John is the best preserved), and its style has the same light but masterful touch seen in Anne's Prayer Book. The leaf can thus be dated to around the same time, the mid-1490s. Furthermore, the *bâtarde* script of the Philadelphia leaf is quite close to that of the Prayer Book; close enough, indeed, that both could easily be by the same

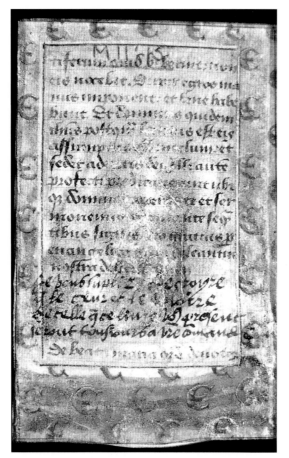

Fig. 19. Jean Poyet, border of *E*s, on a single leaf from a Book of Hours; France, Tours, mid-1490s. Philadelphia, Free Library, Rare Book Department, Lewis E M11:15a (recto).

Fig. 20. Jean Poyet, Lamentation, on a single leaf from a Book of Hours; France, Tours, mid-1490s. Philadelphia, Free Library, Rare Book Department, Lewis E M11:15a (verso).

scribe. The dimensions of the leaf are small enough to qualify as being from a *"petites heures."* Most intriguing are the *E*s that are peppered onto the border of the recto of the leaf. It is significant that these *E*s decorate a plain text page (the end of Mark's Gospel). This hints at the possibility, if not the probability, that all of the text pages throughout the original codex were so treated, resulting in a (small but) luxurious volume that might then easily accommodate the 271 borders tallied in the payment document. As for the *E*s themselves, could they not be part of a set of letters spelling Anne's name like the initials in the borders of her Prayer Book? Finally, there is the French inscription that was added to the recto. It reads:

> *Je vous suplie de croyre*
> *Q[ue] le ceur et le gloire*
> *De celle q[ui] ce livre vo[us] present*
> *Seront tousiours a v[ot]re com[m]ande*

28

I beg you to believe
that the heart and the glory
of the woman who presents this book to you
will always be at your command.

The script is typically French from the early sixteenth century; this dedicatory inscription thus reveals that sometime soon after the book was made, it was given away as a gift by its female owner. Intriguingly, the script itself—by an unprofessional hand—compares very closely to Anne's own handwriting (as in, for example, a letter from Anne to Louis XII prior to their marriage; Paris, Bibliothèque Nationale de France, MS Bèthune 8465, fol. 10). The inscription, in other words, could be by Anne herself.

Unfortunately, the evidence presented by the Philadelphia leaf is not sufficient to reach absolutely firm conclusions. But there are enough intriguing intersections between the leaf and Anne's Prayer Book—artist, style, calligraphy, size, border letters, and, potentially, the same patron—to raise the possibility that the leaf represents a fragment from the Book of Hours that the 1497 document tells us Poyet painted for the queen. If this can ultimately be proven, any questions about connecting the body of work associated with Poyet and the artist himself become moot.

Tilliot Hours

The next work that should be discussed is the Tilliot Hours because it combines aspects of both the early work of Poyet from the 1480s and the mature work of the 1490s (London, British Library, Yates Thompson MS 5). Named after an eighteenth-century owner (Jean Bénigne Lucotte, seigneur du Tilliot), the book can be dated to around 1500. (A previously unnoticed detail that helps confirm this relative date is the presence of rather boisterous scrolls in the four borders of the evangelists. These are closely related to—and were probably inspired by—the scrolls Poyet more logically employs in two copies of Pierre Louis de Valtan's *Commentary on the Apostles' Creed,* manuscripts that, as discussed below, can be dated to shortly before 1498 and to 1500, respectively). The Tilliot Hours is richly decorated with thirteen large and four small miniatures and twenty-five historiated initials. Iconographically, too, it is rich, for the large miniatures are expanded thematically with ancillary scenes in the bottom borders. Thus the Betrayal is complemented by a border depicting Christ before Pilate (for the Passion according to John, fol. 13), the Annunciation by the Fall of Mankind (for Matins of the Hours of the Virgin, fol. 20), the Visitation by the Naming of John the Baptist (for Lauds of the Virgin, fol. 32; fig. 21), and so forth. Using the bottom borders for scenes is an improvement over the rather bored putti who occupy many of the architectural borders in the Hours of Mary of England. The figures in the Tilliot Hours, like those in the Prayer Book and the Hours of Mary of England, are the elegant, graceful figures Poyet developed in the 1490s, but the brushwork here is not as quick nor the palette as light. Poyet, it is clear, could—and did—vary his style. Many of the compositions involve the complicated, but always clear, spaces that the artist had already mastered in the Briçonnet Hours. In the Visitation, for example, the patio in the foreground where the Virgin and Elizabeth meet is clearly defined by the floor tiles and the wall behind the figures (fig. 21). The middle ground is defined by the tall building at the left and by the man with the walking stick who crosses through it. And, finally, the background is filled by a domed structure, covered with architectural detail, in which the birth of John the Baptist takes place. As a whole the Tilliot Hours is a very satisfying book to hold and behold (because of its stylistic beauty and iconographic richness, its illuminator is sometimes called the Master of the Tilliot Hours by those who are shy of the name Jean Poyet).

Fig. 21. Jean Poyet, Visitation and Naming of John the Baptist, from the "Tilliot Hours"; France, Tours, c. 1500. London, British Library, Yates Thompson MS 5, fol. 32.

Hours of Henry VIII

If, in the Tilliot Hours, Poyet revisits some of the grander elements of his earlier style, in two manuscripts in the Pierpont Morgan Library, both datable to around 1500, he returns to it, but in the process both updates and refashions it. The first manuscript is the subject of the present facsimile, the Hours of Henry VIII. It is truly a grand manuscript, larger (at 10⅛ x 7⅛ in., that is, 25.6 x 18 cm) than any of the books discussed so far and, with fifty-five miniatures, the richest. As opposed to those of the Tilliot Hours, the compositions here are truly monumental, an effect achieved by increasing the size of the figures relative to their surroundings. The perspective in many of the miniatures, too, helps reveal the justification behind Poyet's fame in this realm. The elegance of the spatial clarity of the Annunciation (fol. 30v), for example, is a tour de force where space flows seamlessly from a clearly defined interior into a neatly laid out garden, then to a distant cityscape, and, finally, to a horizon filled with faraway hills. Poyet's equally skilled handling of pure landscape, as in the Jerome in Penance (fol. 170) or in the Calendar miniatures, harks back to that seen in the Loches triptych (see fig. 16). The palette, while darker and denser than that of the pastel-dominated Prayer Book, does not return to the heaviness or opacity of the Briçonnet Hours. Lighter tones are mixed with the darker. Many of the miniatures, including the twelve Calendar scenes and all but one of the Suffrages, have borders filled with related figures or vignettes. Unlike the borders in the Tilliot Hours, these are executed in monochrome tones, highlighted with gold, the colors of which are a wonderful range of brown, blue, green, oxblood, slate, rust, and plum. These borders are the work of shop assistants; differences from one to the other reflect a healthy number of participants active within the Poyet atelier.

Missal of Guillaume Lallemant

The second Morgan manuscript painted in this grand manner is the Missal of Guillaume Lallemant (MS M.495). Including the Lallemant family arms no fewer than eight times, this Missal was probably made for Guillaume Lallemant, who was a canon and archdeacon of Tours; the manuscript is made for Tours use. It has been variously dated, from circa 1495 to 1510–15, but there are no good reasons to date it anywhere but near (if perhaps after) the Hours of Henry VIII, to which it compares stylistically. Poyet painted the Missal's five large miniatures, one historiated initial, one historiated border, and all the minor dec-

Fig. 22. Jean Poyet, Resurrection, from the "Missal of Guillaume Lallemant"; France, Tours, c. 1500. New York, Pierpont Morgan Library, MS M.495, fol. 50v.

oration (numerous foliate initials and line endings). The Resurrection is particularly impressive (fig. 22). A rush of motion is implied by the asymmetrical composition in which Christ hovers in the air off to the right, above a path leading through the garden. The Savior's miraculous departure from the sealed tomb awakens the three sleepy guards, who stare at the flying figure in wonder. As François Avril has observed, the monumental composition reveals Poyet's debts to Mantegna. The remaining eighteen small miniatures are not by Poyet nor, curiously, by anyone in his shop. They are by the Master of Spencer 6, so called after a Book of Hours with that shelf number in the New York Public Library. This artist, however, seems to have been active in Bourges, a city in which the patron, Guillaume Lallemant, was also a canon. The presence of different artists within the manuscript is not necessarily evidence that there was a real collaboration between the two. As already mentioned, Poyet had painted all the minor decoration throughout the manuscript and then executed all the large miniatures. He was starting on the smaller pictures (he finished one historiated initial and an elaborate border) when, as I see it, the Missal was pulled from his hands by an impatient canon who had the work completed on one of his sojourns in Bourges. The vast difference in style between Poyet and the Spencer Master, and the rather cavalier manner in which the Bourges painter sometimes covered over parts of Poyet's initials with his own boisterous borders, would indicate the two artists were not actually in direct contact.

In 1997, Dr. Robert Fuchs and Dr. Doris Oltrogge, both professors in the conservation department of the Fachhochschule in Cologne, visited the Morgan Library and examined the Lallemant Missal. Using portable instruments, Fuchs and Oltrogge combined the process of reflectography (using infrared, ultraviolet, and visible lights) with band-pass filters. Their examination met with success and, in a number of cases, revealed elaborate underdrawings beneath the miniatures (fig. 23). These underdrawings reveal the hand of a master who was able to work up compositions directly on the vellum, sketching in figures at will. The lively lines, indicative of the creative act

Fig. 23. Jean Poyet, Resurrection (detail of underdrawing), from the "Missal of Guillaume Lallemant"; France, Tours, c. 1500. New York, Pierpont Morgan Library, MS M.495, fol. 50v.

Fig. 24. Jean Poyet, *Sacrifice of Isaac,* drawing; France, Tours, c. 1500. London, British Museum, Department of Drawings, acc. no. 1874-6-13-539.

Fig. 25. Jean Poyet, *Coronation of King David,* drawing; France, Tours, c. 1500. American private collection.

Fig. 26. Jean Poyet, Virgin and Child, single leaf from a Book of Hours; France, Tours, c. 1500. Paris, Musée du Louvre, Département des Arts Graphiques, R.F. 3890.

(but not acceptable to fifteenth-century French eyes), would be covered over in the painting process. The reclining soldier reproduced here from the Resurrection shows how Poyet thought of his figures in the Italian manner, conceiving the nude form before clothing it (fig. 23). The legs of the soldier, clearly indicated in the under-drawing, are much less discernible in the finished miniature. The discovery of under-drawings in the Lallemant Missal is particularly felicitous because their sketchy style relates closely to a set of five drawings (today in four different collections) that have been attributed to Poyet. The *Sacrifice of Isaac* is typical of the group (fig. 24). While the execution in this sheet (as well as the others; fig. 25) is slightly more finished than that of the underdrawings in the Lallemant Missal, the hand is the same; the developed landscape, the clever use of foreground, middle ground, and background spaces, and the contrapposto figures are all characteristic of Poyet's mature style.

Single Leaf of the Virgin and Child

The last of Poyet's major works to be discussed is a single leaf of the Virgin and Child (Paris, Musée du Louvre, Département des Arts Graphiques, R.F. 3890; fig. 26).

Fig. 27. Jean Poyet and his workshop, Four Seasons, from a manuscript of the *Secret des secrets* and Alain Chartier's *Bréviaire des nobles;* France, Tours, c. 1490. Paris, Bibliothèque Nationale de France, MS n. a. fr. 18145, fol. 50.

Fig. 28. Jean Poyet, King Charles VIII Presented by Mary Magdalene to the Resurrected Christ, from a Book of Hours; France, Tours, c. 1494–95. New York, Pierpont Morgan Library, MS M.250, fol. 14.

Remnants of text indicate that the miniature was on the verso of the leaf and introduced the beginning of the Hours of the Virgin from a Book of Hours. The large size (9 3/16 x 6 3/4 in., that is, 23.4 x 17.2 cm) and monumental style of the painting make it the sole surviving fragment of what was once a truly magnificent manuscript. The nearly monochromatic niche in which the Virgin sits sets off the color juxtapositions that are typical for Poyet but handled here with utmost subtlety. The grayish green of the lining of the Virgin's hood is set against the robin's egg blue of the lining of the cloak, which, in turn, is contrasted with the rose of the robe. The pale gold of the Virgin's sash and the grayish white of the Christ Child's coverlet continue these playful juxtapositions. In style, though, this illumination is a little different from both the small fine manner of Anne's Prayer Book and the Hours of Mary of England and the grand manner of the Hours of Henry VIII and the Lallemant Missal. In fact, the style of the Louvre Madonna is a wonderful combination of the two manners where areas of stippled paint contrast with areas of dense, opaque application.

Minor Works

There are a number of works by Poyet that, although minor and often involving participation of the workshop, deserve mention because they offer anchors for dating his oeuvre. Three works are from the reign of Charles VIII (r. 1483–98). The first is a kind of instructional manual for rulers; it contains two texts, the *Secret des secrets* and Alain Chartier's *Bréviaire des nobles* (Paris, Bibliothèque Nationale de France, MS n. a. fr. 18145; fig. 27). Charles is the last king mentioned in a listing of the French rulers, so the work apparently comes from the time of his reign. A date of 1490–95 has been suggested, but the late 1480s or around 1490 seems to fit both the opacity of the palette and the costume details better. A third good reason to keep this manuscript in this earlier time period is that Charles was still a teenager, in need of royal *exempla;* he did not assume active rulership until 1492. Together, these two treatises of moralizing instruction are illustrated by twenty-two miniatures by Poyet and his shop. The second work from Charles's reign is a bifolio with a full-page image of the king's arms and, facing it, a miniature of Charles VIII Presented to the Resurrected Christ by Mary Magdalene (New York, Pierpont Morgan Library, MS M.250, fols. 13v–14; fig. 28). The pictures, apparently created for the king himself, have been dated to around 1494–95, the time when Charles began to use the title of King of Sicily and Jerusalem (which is inscribed below each image). The miniatures are inserted into a rather motley Book of Hours that dates, however, to the early sixteenth century, so

Fig. 29. Jean Poyet, St. Peter Composing the First Article of Faith, from Pierre Louis de Valtan's *Super qualibet dictione symboli apostolici;* France, Tours, c. 1495–98. London, British Library, Add. MS 35320, fol. 4.

the original context of their commission remains a mystery. The third manuscript from Charles's reign is a copy of Pierre Louis de Valtan's *Super qualibet dictione symboli apostolici* (London, British Library, Add. MS 35320). This manuscript of de Valtan's *Commentary on the Apostles' Creed* was the presentation copy to Charles, and its frontispiece shows the king accepting the volume from its kneeling author. This miniature, which is not by Poyet (although he might have had something to do with its underdrawing), is fol-

Fig. 30. Workshop of Jean Poyet, Annunciation, from a *Psaultier abregié;* France, Tours, probably 1498. Paris, Bibliothèque Nationale de France, MS lat. 2844, fol. 12.

Fig. 31. Jean Poyet, St. Matthew Composing the Ninth Article of Faith, from Pierre Louis de Valtan's *Super qualibet dictione symboli apostolici;* France, Tours, 1500. Rotthalmünster, Antiquariat Heribert Tenschert, s.n., fol. 21.

lowed by twelve pictures by Poyet showing the evangelists composing their Articles of Faith (fig. 29). On the basis of style and its relation to a second copy of the text (see below), this manuscript can be dated between about 1495 and Charles's death in 1498.

A slender prayer book of only thirteen folios, whose prologue calls it a *"psaultier abregié,"* is thought to have belonged to Anne de Bretagne during the brief period of her widowhood, between 8 April 1498 and 8 January 1499 (Paris, Bibliothèque Nationale de France, MS lat. 2844; fig. 30). The manuscript's decoration—miniatures, initials, line endings—is entirely in grisaille highlighted with gold. The *cordelière,* alternating with an acanthus, appears in every other line ending and in three of the main borders. Certain phrases within the prayers suggest that the book was destined for royal hands: the Virgin is addressed as *"Souveraine dame"* at the beginning (fol. 1v) and, in a final prayer, as *"Princesse tant belle plaisante et fine"* (fol. 13). Interestingly, this last prayer uses the phrase, *"la grace divine du roy ihus vostre bon pere et filz,"* thus mentioning the Virgin's peculiar relationship to God, who was both her father and her son. In her widowhood, at least after August when she committed to the marriage with Louis, Anne was between a pair of husbands who, symbolically speaking, were father and son. The manuscript was illuminated by Poyet's workshop.

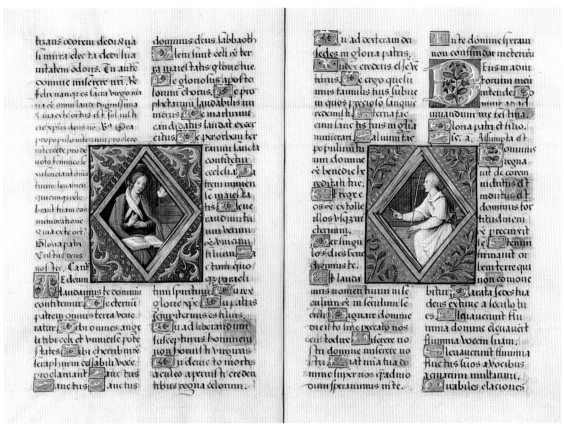

Fig. 32. Jean Poyet, Annunciation, from a Book of Hours; France, Tours, c. 1500. Copenhagen, Kongelige Bibliotek, MS Thott 541 4°, fols. 17v–18 (Virgin Annunciate actually on fol. 14v and Gabriel on fol. 22).

The last of the minor but datable manuscripts by Poyet is a second copy of de Valtan's *Super qualibet dictione symboli apostolici* (Rotthalmünster, Antiquariat Heribert Tenschert). This manuscript, a sister to Charles VIII's presentation copy in the British Library, comes from the reign of King Louis XII (r. 1498–1515). It, too, contains a suite of twelve miniatures of the apostles by Poyet (fig. 31). It was given by de Valtan to Queen Isabella the Catholic when he was envoy to Spain for Louis XII; the manuscript is inscribed with the date of its presentation, 19 November 1500 *("XIII kaleñ. Decembres anno dominice nativitatis et sacri iubilei Millesimo Quingentesimo")*.

A final minor work should be discussed, even though it offers no clues for dating Poyet's oeuvre. The manuscript is a Book of Hours with only sixteen small miniatures, but their arrangement within this specially designed codex makes for an especially charming volume (Copenhagen, Kongelige Bibliotek, MS Thott 541 4°). The miniatures are arranged in pairs, one set of which is always visible (beginning after the Calendar) throughout the book, seen through diamond-shaped holes cut into the leaves (fig. 32). Thus, while reading the Gospel Lessons, *"Obsecro te,"* and *"O intemerata"* (fols. 6v–10v, followed by textless fols. 11–14), one continually sees the two miniatures of John on Patmos (which is on fol. 6v) and the Virgin and Child (fol. 14). While praying

Matins and Lauds of the Hours of the Virgin, the miniatures of the Virgin Annunciate (fol. 14v) and Gabriel (fol. 22) were always visible (fig. 32). Throughout Prime, Terce, Sext, None, and Vespers, one viewed the miniatures of the Nativity (fol. 22v) and the Flight into Egypt (fol. 30). While reading Compline, the weekday and Advent variations, John's Passion, and the *"Stabat mater,"* one could meditate on a picture of the Assumption of the Virgin (fol. 30v) or Christ's Agony in the Garden (fol. 46). Throughout the Penitential Psalms and Litany, one continually witnessed David (fol. 46v) leering at the bathing Bathsheba (fol. 53). While praying the Hours of the Cross or the Hours of the Holy Spirit, miniatures of Christ's Carrying the Cross (fol. 53v) and Pentecost (fol. 56) were always before one's eyes. Throughout the Office of the Dead one saw Job, seated on his dungheap (fol. 56v), harassed by his tormentors (fol. 72). And, finally, throughout the Suffrages, one glimpsed miniatures of the Trinity (fol. 72v) and of All Saints (fol. 77). There are a number of ruled but blank leaves in the manuscript, including (for example) the wasteful seven blank pages on folios 11 to 14

Fig. 33. Workshop of Jean Poyet, Last Judgment, from a Book of Hours; France, Tours, c. 1490–1500. New York, Pierpont Morgan Library, MS M.388, fol. 109v.

Fig. 34. Workshop of Jean Poyet, Coronation of the Virgin, from a Book of Hours; France, Tours, c. 1490–1500. New York, Pierpont Morgan Library, MS M.9, fol. 83v.

already mentioned (between the *"O intemerata"* and Matins of the Hours of the Virgin). These blanks are numerous enough to indicate the scribe's unfamiliarity and discomfort in laying out this rare type of "peekaboo" *Horae.* The book, of course, was a special commission and clearly an unusual one; Poyet felt compelled to offer his best to his client, so he himself painted all sixteen miniatures. They can be dated on style to around 1500. (Poyet seems to have been responsible for a second peekaboo *Horae,* the so-called Petau Hours, in a Paris private collection; like the Copenhagen manuscript, it has sixteen miniatures, visible in pairs throughout the book after the Calendar. Not having seen the manuscript, however, I cannot comment on its style or position in Poyet's oeuvre.)

Nature of Poyet's Workshop

The manuscripts just discussed involve at times the participation of Poyet's workshop. There is a growing body of work whose close relationship to the Poyet style, sometimes involving participation by the hand of the master himself, con-

Fig. 35. Jean Poyet and his workshop, St. Peter of Luxemburg at Prayer, from a Book of Hours; France, Tours, c. 1490–1500. Baltimore, Walters Art Gallery, MS W.430, fol. 165v.

jures up a picture of a busy shop with many members, but one carefully controlled, for the sake of consistency and quality, by its leader. The five manuscripts discussed directly below can all be dated from the 1490s to around 1500, the period of Poyet's most intense activity. Two Books of Hours in the Morgan Library reflect the range of styles possible within the shop (MSS M.9 and M.388). The hand of manuscript M.388 closely mimics the master's style (fig. 33), while that of manuscript M.9 is much blander (fig. 34). A small Book of Hours in the Walters Art Gallery in Baltimore has connections with many other works by Poyet (MS W.430). Its *bâtarde* script is quite close to the calligraphy of Anne's Prayer Book, and its grisaille echoes that of the *"psaultier abregié"* associated with Anne's widowhood mentioned above. Its borders, too, have those rather boisterous scrolls that Poyet liked to use in some of his margins. Many of this little manuscript's miniatures are shop work, while others (fols. 86, 114 to 165v; fig. 35) are of

Fig. 36. Jean Poyet and his workshop, Job on the Dungheap, from a Book of Hours; France, Tours, c. 1490–1500. Baltimore, Walters Art Gallery, MS W.295, fol. 42v (detail).

Fig. 37. Jean Poyet and his workshop, Trinity, from a Missal; France, Tours, c. 1490–1500. Paris, Bibliothèque Nationale de France, MS lat. 850, fol. 141.

such high quality that they are probably by the master himself. A second Book of Hours in the Walters Art Gallery, of an unusually large folio size (13⅝ x 8¹¹⁄₁₆ in., that is, 34.5 x 22 cm), was apparently used by Poyet to help train his assistants (MS W.295). In at least four of the miniatures Poyet painted the head of one figure, leaving the others and the rest of the composition to be completed by members of the shop. In the Annunciation to the Shepherds (fol. 22), for example, the fine head of the central shepherd is by Poyet, while the other two, much inferior in quality, are by shop hands. In a similar way Poyet is responsible for the head of Simeon in the Presentation (fol. 25v), the left-most apostle in the Pentecost (fol. 33), and the central of Job's tormentors (fol. 42v; fig. 36), whereas the rest of each of the miniatures was finished by the shop. It is an amazing manuscript. The fifth manuscript considered here in relation to Poyet and his shop is a Missal in Paris (Bibliothèque Nationale de France, MS lat. 850). Unlike the large miniatures in the Lallemant Missal, the illumination of the two large and three small miniatures in this manuscript is mostly by Poyet's shop. The master, however, "dropped in," painting, for example, the handsome head of David (fol. 1), the fine faces of Mary and Joseph in the Nativity (fol. 11v), as well as those

of Christ and God the Father in the Trinity (fol. 141; fig. 37). When the last miniature of the book was painted (the Resurrection on fol. 145v), however, Poyet was
gone; the reduction in quality is apparent.

The final manuscript to be discussed in relation to Poyet and his shop is a copy of
the *Chronique martinienne* (Copenhagen, Kongelige Bibliotek, MS Thott 430 2°). The
text is Martin of Troppau's *Chronicon pontificum et imperatorum* (History of the Popes
and Emperors, which stops in 1277) plus additional material that brought the chronicle up to 1394; the translation into French is by Sebastien Mamerot, who, the text
tells us, performed his task in 1458 under the patronage of Louis de Laval. The thick
manuscript has twenty-three large and fifty-eight small miniatures. Poyet designed
and drew most of the large miniatures and painted some (or some part) of them. The
finely executed figure of the Virgin on folio 59, the noble face of St. Gregory on folio
87v, and the Fouquetesque group of soldiers crossing the river on folio 224 are all
evidence of Poyet's "dropping in" and participating in painting (at least) parts of many
of the large miniatures. The small miniature on folio 240v is so fine that it, too, seems
to be by Poyet himself; did he execute it as a model of quality for the other fifty-
seven small pictures? If so, he was not successful, for these miniatures are second-rate
at best; they do not even seem very Poyetesque. What is going on in this book?

Fig. 38. Jean Poyet and his workshop, Fall of Simon Magus, from the *Chronique martinienne;* France, Tours,
c. 1500–1503. Copenhagen, Kongelige Bibliotek, MS Thott 430 2°, fol. 66.

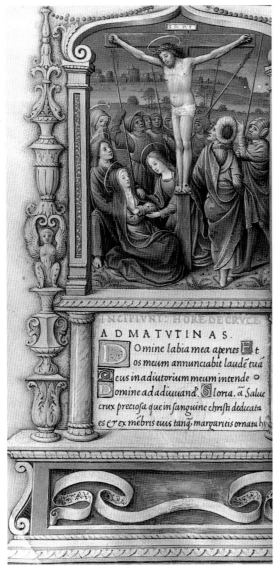

Fig. 39. Master of Claude de France, Crucifixion, from a Book of Hours; France, Tours, c. 1515–20. London, British Library, MS Add. 35315, fol. 47v.

Comparing the *Chronique martini-enne* to the Hours of Henry VIII reveals that the same scribe wrote both (his capitals, best seen in the Calendar of the Hours, are quite distinctive). This fact might help pull the two manuscripts together in date, but not necessarily closely, as scribes, like painters, can live long lives. Further comparison of the *Chronique* to the Hours of Henry VIII, however, reveals at least one composition created for the one reused in the other. The composition of the Fall of Simon Magus in the Hours (fol. 175) reappears in a reduced and not as interesting version in the chronicle (fig. 38). The handsome white dog that appears at the center of the miniature in the Hours is absent from the version in the *Chronique* but appears in the latter codex in a picture on folio 47v. These reworkings date the *Chronique* to shortly after the Hours, that is, between about 1500 (the date of the Hours) and 1503 (the rough date of Poyet's death). This makes it a very late work, possibly the last upon which Poyet participated with members of his shop. The large commission apparently stretched Poyet and his ate-lier, for the rather pedestrian small miniatures were not even painted by someone from the shop, but an illuminator hired from outside to crank out the numerous little pictures in a style, while generically sympathetic to Poyet's, is not, as I have already mentioned, really Poyetesque. Finally, in some of the large minia-tures, a distinctive shop hand can sometimes be identified. The figures with the large noses on the right in the miniature on folio 47v and all of the miniature on folio 178, for example, are the work of this distinctive hand, who, in his ability to imitate his master's style, is clearly Poyet's best shop assistant. This man and his activity in two important Books of Hours created after Poyet's death need now to be discussed.

Book of Hours by the Master of Claude de France and the "pseudo-Poyet"

We must now consider two works pivotal for our understanding of the true nature of Poyet's art, for they touch on the issue of Poyet's putative late career. The later of the two is a Book of Hours that has been seen as a collaborative effort of the Master of Claude de France (whom we encountered in connection with the Hours of Mary of England) and Jean Poyet (London, British Library, Add. MS 35315). For many valid reasons—the period of activity of the Claude Master, the italic script, and the proportions of the book—this manuscript must date between 1515 and 1520. The contribution by the Claude Master (sometimes with assistants) includes the fifteen Calendar borders and six large miniatures (between fols. 1–8v and 47v–66v; fig. 39). The work that has been attributed to Poyet includes the eight miniatures illustrating the Hours of the Virgin (fols. 17 to 41; fig. 40). The manuscript is all of a piece: it was not started by one artist and finished by the other. It is a true collaboration, and even on one miniature, the Annunciation to the Shepherds (fol. 31v), the Claude Master and the Poyetesque hand worked together.

Fig. 40. The "pseudo-Poyet," Annunciation, from a Book of Hours; France, Tours, c. 1515–20. London, British Library, MS Add. 35315, fol. 17.

In relation to Poyet's career, these miniatures are thought to be his last work. But are they really his? The nature of this collaboration—where the Master of Claude de France is actually doing more than his colleague—is a little odd to begin with. Except for the Missal of Guillaume Lallemant, which might not really have been a true joint effort, and the *Chronique martinienne,* in which Poyet hired a hack to paint the manuscript's numerous small miniatures, Poyet did not collaborate. He did not need to, heading, as he did, a workshop populated with assistants trained to imitate him. Scrutiny of the Poyetesque miniatures in Additional 35315 reveals important differences between them and the work already discussed. The purples, blues, and pinks,

43

while typical of the Poyet palette, lack his masterful subtlety, and their juxtapositions no longer tease the eye. Compared with the work of the 1490s, the figures here are proportionately shorter, their heads a little bigger, and their gait less lively and animated. The figures of Gabriel and the Virgin in the Annunciation, among the most convincing in the manuscript, reveal, in the profile of the archangel and in Mary's broad flat nose, the absence of Poyet's hand itself (fig. 40). The hand at work here is revealed by the monochrome figures of Synagoga, Ecclesia, and the male nude lounging on the architectural base; their free, relaxed execution recalls the style of the monochrome borders in the Hours of Henry VIII, the style of the borders in the Lallemant Missal (see fig. 22), and some of the miniatures in the *Chronique martinienne*. In other words, the artist who painted the Poyetesque miniatures in Additional 35315 is not Poyet himself, but his best shop assistant. This "pseudo-Poyet," while good, was never as good as the master himself. Awkwardnesses multiply in the other miniatures. In the Visitation (fol. 25v), Mary's poor posture makes her look like a hunchback, and Elizabeth's masculine face makes her look like a man in drag. The "pseudo-Poyet" also lacked the finesse of his teacher in his compositions. The cave with two openings, featured in both the Nativity and the Adoration of the Magi (fols. 29v, 33v), is poorly handled in both scenes; in each case the pillar of rock that forms the cave's double entrance divides the scene very uncomfortably. A column in the middle of the Presentation (fol. 35v) clumsily hides both Simeon's and Christ's outstretched hands.

Hours of Jean Lallemant the Elder and the "pseudo-Poyet"

The second major manuscript in which the "pseudo-Poyet" worked is the Hours of Jean Lallemant the Elder (he is possibly the brother of Guillaume). This book has had a curious and confusing history. Already dismembered by the end of the sixteenth century, it survives in three known fragments: London, British Library, Additional MS 39641 (41 fols. with six miniatures); Baltimore, Walters Art Gallery, MS W.459 (33 fols. with one miniature); and Cambridge, Fitzwilliam Museum, Marlay Cutting, Fr. 7 (single leaf with one miniature). Other parts of the manuscript disappeared as recently as this century (and may turn up again). As is often typical with the Lallemant family's esoteric taste, Jean's manuscript was an unusual commission. Each large miniature was double-framed, first by an Italianate architectural structure and then, farther out onto the margin, by a primitive construction of tree trunks (figs. 41, 42). Unusual, too, for its time were the manuscript's Calendar cycle of full-page labors of the months and subjects rarely found in *Horae*, such as the Baptism of Christ and the Resurrected Christ's Appearance to His Mother. Of the surviving fragments the "pseudo-Poyet" painted only three miniatures, all in the London portion (fols. 3v, 19v, 41v; fig. 41). The other miniatures (including the ones in Baltimore and Cambridge plus the lost twelve Calendar scenes, which can be judged from reproductions) are by the Master of Morgan 85 (fig. 42), an artist (named after a

Book of Hours in the Morgan Library) who was chief assistant to the prolific Parisian artist Jean Pichore (fl. c. 1502–20). The Lallemant Hours can be dated to the early sixteenth century. As with Additional 35315, the "pseudo-Poyet" plays the role of collaborator in the manuscript and, in this case, a subordinate one, having painted far fewer miniatures than his colleague, the Morgan 85 Master. Poyet himself would never have played such a subsidiary role. Furthermore, there are awkwardnesses, as seen in Additional 35315, that are even more evident in this earlier work, such as in the Resurrected Christ Appearing to Mary (fig. 41). The parenthesis-like form of Christ is not a very convincing figure. He stands with his weight evenly distributed on both legs—Poyet, who loved contrapposto, avoided such stances. The Virgin has the same flat, broad nose seen in the later book, Additional 35315. Behind the figures, the architecture features a wall, the passage through which is too impossibly narrow for even the resurrected Christ to walk! The landscape, furthermore, lacks any of Poyet's poetry. In the scene of David Chastised by Nathan (fol. 3v), there are

Fig. 41. The "pseudo-Poyet," Resurrected Christ Appearing to His Mother, from the "Hours of Jean Lallemant the Elder"; France, Paris, c. 1510–20. London, British Library, Add. MS 39641, fol. 41v.

Fig. 42. Master of Morgan 85, Last Judgment, from the "Hours of Jean Lallemant the Elder"; France, Paris, c. 1510–20. London, British Library, Add. MS 39641, fol. 1.

45

further awkward moments. Both David's crown and his harp lie on the ground in very odd, unconvincing ways.

Some authors have dated the Lallemant Hours to around 1498, while others more convincingly put it into the sixteenth century. If Poyet was indeed dead by 1503, this manuscript could have been the first major venture, near or after the death of the master, on the part of his chief assistant—the "pseudo-Poyet." It is worth remembering that the 1498 document is the last record of Poyet's name. That fact, plus the examination of the two Books of Hours just discussed, does offer some indication that the artist himself did, indeed, disappear sometime in the early sixteenth century. As a result, the "pseudo-Poyet" was forced to collaborate with others, for after Poyet's death, he would have been a free, independent painter but not the overseer of a busy shop. He would have been on his own and, as such, would not have been in a position of control vis-à-vis the commissions he received.

Fig. 43. Follower of Jean Poyet, Death of Tommasina Spinola, from Jean d'Auton's *Complainte sur la mort de dame Thomassine Espinolle;* France, Tours?, 1505. Paris, Bibliothèque Nationale de France, MS fr. 1684, fol. 7v.

The Disintegration of Poyet's Workshop

Finally, there are two manuscripts that help flesh out our picture of the disintegration of Poyet's workshop after his death. Although the "pseudo-Poyet" was his best pupil, there were certainly others, less gifted, who also struck out on their own. Two manuscripts of Jean d'Auton's *Complainte sur la mort de dame Thomassine Espinolle* are each illustrated with three miniatures by an artist who was once a member of Poyet's shop (Paris, Bibliothèque Nationale de France, MSS fr. 1684 and fr. 25419). The artist of these two volumes, who is clearly a person different from the "pseudo-Poyet," employs some of Poyet's figural style and facial physiognomies but little of his palette and none of his painting technique (fig. 43). Tommasina Spinola, as the text tells us, was the *"entendyo"* (chivalric favorite) of Louis XII; each manuscript has a suite of miniatures depicting

Tommasina Pining for Louis at the Docks of Genoa, the Death of Tommasina, and Louis XII in Mourning. The manuscripts can be dated to 1505, the date when rumors of Tommasina's death (supposedly in reaction to false rumors in Italy of Louis's death during his illness at this time) were circulating at the French court. The quality of their illumination is so mediocre that they could never have been generated from Poyet's shop were he still alive. Their creator, like the "pseudo-Poyet," must also have become an independent artist at the same time and for the same reason, the death of Poyet.

Conclusion

A reexamination of both the textual evidence (documents and literary sources) and the main art works attributed to Jean Poyet suggests a picture of the artist and his career that is close to that described by earlier scholarship but now further refined. Two distinct stylistic phases can be discerned, one early (from the 1480s to the early '90s), the other mature (from the 1490s to around 1500). The art that had previously been construed as his late work is by his main shop assistant (designated here the "pseudo-Poyet"); his is a good but inferior hand. The general chronology is supported by the lack of Poyet's name in documents beyond 1498 and the literary source suggesting a death date by 1503. Additionally, there is no art that can be given to the artist we call Jean Poyet past the very early sixteenth century. Poyet's death by 1503 would explain the dispersal of members of his shop and the diminished quality of work done without his direct control.

Certain discoveries, we hope, have also contributed to our knowledge of Poyet's oeuvre. The pedagogical function of Anne de Bretagne's Prayer Book and the concomitant identification of its male portrait as Charles-Orland help anchor the date of the manuscript between 1492 and '95. The identification of the Briçonnet arms in the Haarlem manuscript offers another reason other than style to connect the Hours to Tours, hometown of this famous family. And a single leaf in the Free Library of Philadelphia has a good chance of being the sole surviving fragment from the lost 1497 *"petites heures"* of Anne de Bretagne.

Plates and Commentaries for the Hours of Henry VIII

CALENDAR

(fols. 1–6v)

Calendars in Books of Hours do not tell time by enumerating the days of the month (from January 1 to 31, for example), but by listing the important liturgical feasts of the month. Most of these holy days consist of saints' days, with his or her name usually followed by an abbreviation indicating whether the saint is priest (*Felicis presb[ite]ri,* January 14), abbot (*Mauri abb[at]is,* January 15), martyr (*Marcelli m[arty]r[is],* January 16), virgin (*Prisce virg[in]is,* January 18), and so forth. Many feasts are octaves, a commemoration of the end of an eight-day celebration (such as the Octave of St. Stephen Protomartyr on January 2). And, finally, some feasts commemorate events, such as the Circumcision of Christ (January 1), the Epiphany (January 6), or the Translation (removal from one place to another) of the Relics of St. Martin (January 31). The majority of the year's feasts are written in brown ink, but the more important ones are in red or blue (they more or less alternate). This Calendar has many blank spaces, which is also common in *Horae;* these "blank" days had no special feast so, at church, the Mass of the preceding Sunday was recited.

At the left of each of the two columns of feasts is a series of letters, beginning with *"A"* and running through *"G,"* that starts on January 1 and ends with December 31. These are the so-called Dominical Letters, which are used to designate Sundays throughout the year. At the beginning of each year, for instance, the reader would know that every *F* was a Sunday. Because the year has 365 days, the Dominical Letter changed every year, falling back one each time (and, in each leap year, the Letter changed yet again on February 25).

Next to the column of Dominical Letters are a series of Roman numerals from *"i"* to *"xix"* that seem to run in a random order. These are the Golden Numbers, so called because they help the reader determine the date of the movable feast of Easter. The Golden Number, which changes each year, indicates the occurrence of new moons and, counting forward fourteen days, full moons throughout the year. (Using the Dominical Letters, the Golden Numbers, and some rather complicated computations, the reader could find the date of Easter, which is celebrated on the Sunday following the first full moon that falls on or after the vernal equinox.) A two-line inscription at the top of each month tells the reader how many days the month has and how many days the moon has. For example, "January has 31 days; the moon has 30" (*Januari[us] h[abet] d[ies] xxxi. Luna xxx.*). Lunar months are always shorter than the regular months, and the lunar year completes itself in the equivalent of 354 solar days. Lunar years run in cycles that repeat themselves every nineteen years, which means that a particular new moon will only reappear in the same place in the sky once in nineteen years; hence, nineteen Golden Numbers. Each month begins with a large *"KL"* that stands for *"Kalens,"* or, the first of each month. This is the only remnant of the ancient Roman calendrical system that survives in Renaissance Books of Hours.

When Calendars in *Horae* were illustrated, they followed a tradition of depicting two vignettes in each month: the sign of the zodiac and the labor of the month (the activity, usually agrarian, commonly undertaken in the season). By the late fifteenth century, over the course of some 300 years of the history of Books of Hours, these illustrated labors assumed a larger role in the book, literally increasing in size. The labors in the Hours of Henry VIII are nearly half a page and in their horizontal format include much detail and a lot of space. The Calendar of this manuscript is also unusual with its inclusion, in the borders, of some of the saints whose feasts are listed for each month. These vignettes usually illustrate the more important feasts—those written in red or blue ink.

—R.S.W. & K.M.H.

January: Feasting and Keeping Warm (fol. 1)

While a heavy snow covers the land and little can be done in terms of cultivation, the main task to be undertaken in January is to keep well fed and indoors. Having taken a few logs from the snow-covered woodpile, a laborer is about to enter the manor's great hall. Inside, the lord of the house sits, his back to the hearth, in front of his meal. His wife, closer to the fire, warms her hands.

The borders illustrate some of January's major feasts. At the left, reading from top to bottom, are the Circumcision (feast on January 1), the Apostle John (his octave is January 3), and the Adoration of the Magi (Epiphany, January 6). The right border includes Sts. Anthony Abbot (January 17), Sebastian (January 20), Agnes (January 21), Emerentiana (Agnes's foster sister; January 23), and a generic male saint. Without attribute, this and other generic saints within the Calendar's border do not represent particular saints but refer, in a general way, to the virgins and martyrs listed in the month. The zodiacal sign is Aquarius, the Water Carrier.

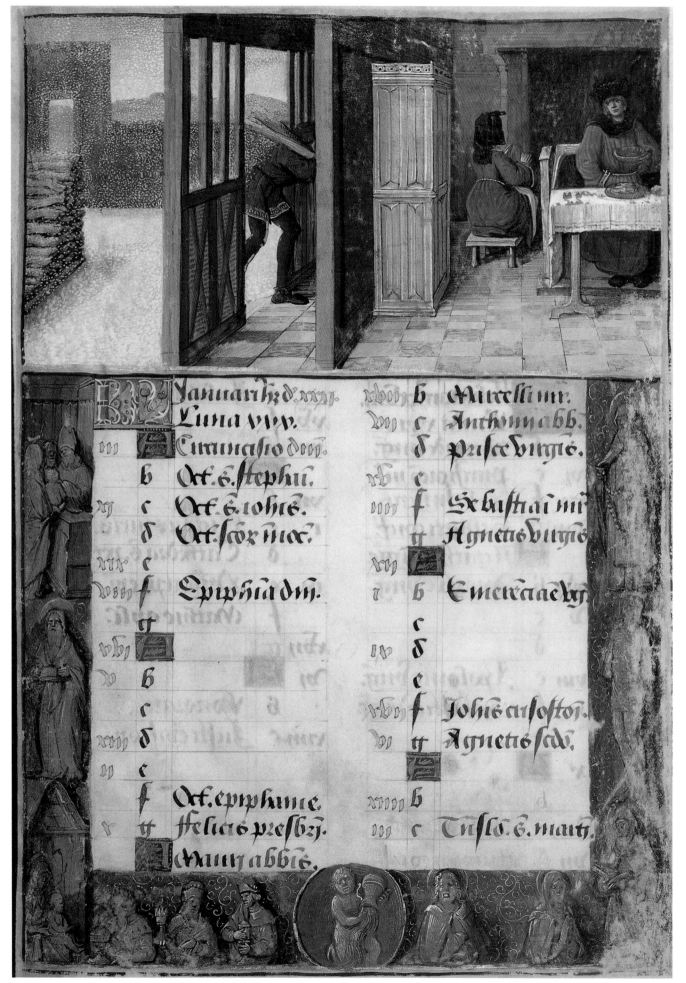

Januarius d̄ xxij.
Luna xxx.

iiij		Circūcisio deī.	xbiij	b	Marcelli mr.
	b	Oct̄. s̄. Stephni.	biij	c	Anthonii abb.
xj	c	Oct̄. s̄. Iohis.		d	Prisce virgis.
	d	Oct̄. scōr ̄ māc.	xbj	e	
xix	e		iiij	f	Sebastiai mr.
bij	f	Epiphīa dm̄.		g	Agnetis virgīs
	g		xij		
xbj			j	b	Emerēciane
b	b			c	
	c		ix	d	
xiij	d			e	
ij	e		xbij	f	Iohīs crisostoī.
	f	Oct̄. epīphanie.	bj	g	Agnetis scd̄o.
x	g	Felicis presbri.			
		Mauri abbis.	xiiij	b	
			iij	c	Tr̄slō. s̄. maurī.

fol. 1v

February: Keeping Warm (fol. 1v)

February's labor is not much different from January's. The lord of the house, richly dressed in fur-lined garments and hat, raises the folds of his clothes, the better to warm his backside. His attention has been caught by his servant, who enters with flagons of wine.

In the left border are the Virgin holding the Christ Child (for the Feast of the Purification, February 2) and Sts. Blaise (holding his attribute, an iron comb, February 3), Agatha, whose breasts are being removed (February 5), and a generic male saint. At the right are Sts. Peter, shown seated and blessing (for the feast of the Chair of St. Peter the Apostle, February 22), and Matthew the Apostle (February 24). The next saint, a bishop, might be any one of the three bishop saints listed for the second half of the month: Polycarp (February 23), Honoratus (February 27; although his feast here may be confused with that of St. Honorine), or Justus (February 28). The last, rather generic, saint may represent the martyr Victor (February 21). The zodiacal sign is Pisces, the Fish.

March: Pruning (fol. 2)

In the early spring month of March, work begins outdoors. The typical labor for the month is the pruning of the vineyard. Workers trim the leafless vines and tie them to the grape arbor. In the foreground is a wood cask for drink.

The figures in the margins begin at the left with St. Albinus (March 1), the Forty Holy Martyrs (March 9), the Mass of St. Gregory (for the Feast of St. Gregory, March 12), and St. Longinus (March 15). On the right are Sts. Benedict (March 21) and Helena (her feast on May 22 has been mistakenly entered here on March 31) and the Annunciation (March 25). The zodiacal sign is Aries, the Ram.

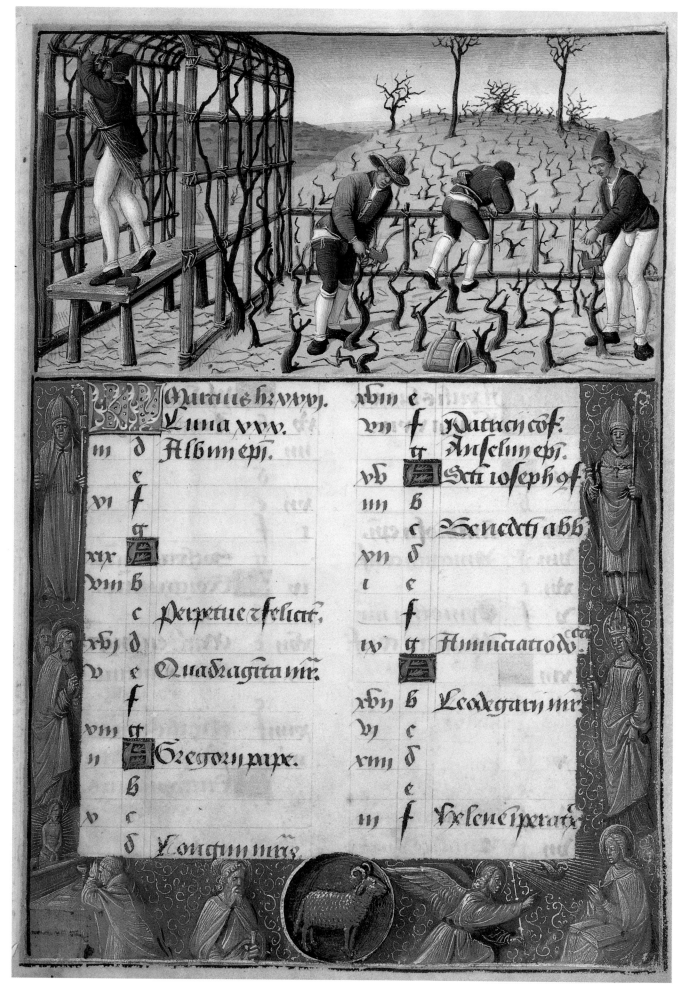

fol. 2

April: Picking Flowers and Making Wreaths (fol. 2v)

In April, the landscape is green and alive. The month's activity is not laborious, but one for the leisure class. A foppishly dressed youth, his hands filled with freshly picked spring flowers, waits while his lady friend weaves the blossoms into a garland.

In the left border is St. Ambrose (April 4), followed by four generic male saints who probably represent the four male saints listed for the first half of the month: Vincent Ferrer (April 5), Timothy (April 7), Macarius (April 8), and Tiburtius (April 14). At the right appear Sts. George, shown slaying the dragon (April 23), Mark the Evangelist (April 25), Eutropius, shown with the ax that killed him through his head (April 30), and Peter Martyr, stabbed in the chest with a dagger, his attribute (April 29). The zodiacal sign is Taurus, the Bull.

May: Picking Branches (fol. 3)

Another leisurely couple perform May's pleasure, the gathering, on the first of the month, of flowering or leafing branches.

In the left border are Sts. Philip and James (May 1), and the True Cross (for the Feast of the Finding of the True Cross, May 3). Next is a generic saint whose presence probably refers to one of the three martyrs listed in the first half of the month: Gordian (May 10), Pancratius (May 12), or Boniface (May 14). The last saint, a monk, is probably the last listed in the first column, Bernard (May 15). At the right are Sts. Bernardine of Siena (the feast of the translation of his relics is on May 17; his regular feast is on May 20) and a bishop or abbot saint. Next are a pope saint (who could refer to any or all of the four pope saints listed: Urbanus I on May 25, Elutherius on May 26, John I on May 27, and Felix I on May 30), another generic male saint, and Petronilla (May 31). The zodiacal sign is Gemini, the Twins (shown in a naked embrace).

fol. 3v

June: Mowing (fol. 3v)

The hard labors of the summer begin in June with the mowing of the hay. At the left, three men rhythmically attack the field with large scythes. Two women rake the loose hay into stacks. Behind them, a wagon waits to be filled. In the foreground at the right are the workers' bundles of food and casks of drink.

In the left border are Sts. Marcellinus (June 2), Barnabas the Apostle (holding a lance, June 11), and three generic figures who can represent any of the six male saints listed after Barnabas. At the right are Sts. John the Baptist (feast of his Nativity on June 24), Eligius (June 25), a generic male saint, and Peter and Paul (June 29). The zodical sign is Cancer, the Crab.

July: Reaping (fol. 4)

The summer harvest continues in July with the reaping of the wheat. Four men, minimally dressed to keep cool, carefully cut the stalks with sickles and lay them in neat bundles. As in June, the foreground features, almost like a still life, their containers of food and drink.

The first two generic figures in the left border resemble apostles and probably illustrate the two octaves (of John on July 1, and Peter and Paul on July 6). Following them are Elizabeth and the Virgin (for the Feast of the Visitation, July 9) and two generic male saints. At the right are Sts. Margaret, shown emerging from the dragon (July 20), Mary Magdalene, holding her ointment jar (July 22), Christopher, carrying Christ on his back, and James, as a pilgrim (July 25), and Anne instructing the Virgin (July 26). The zodiacal sign is Leo, the Lion.

fol. 4

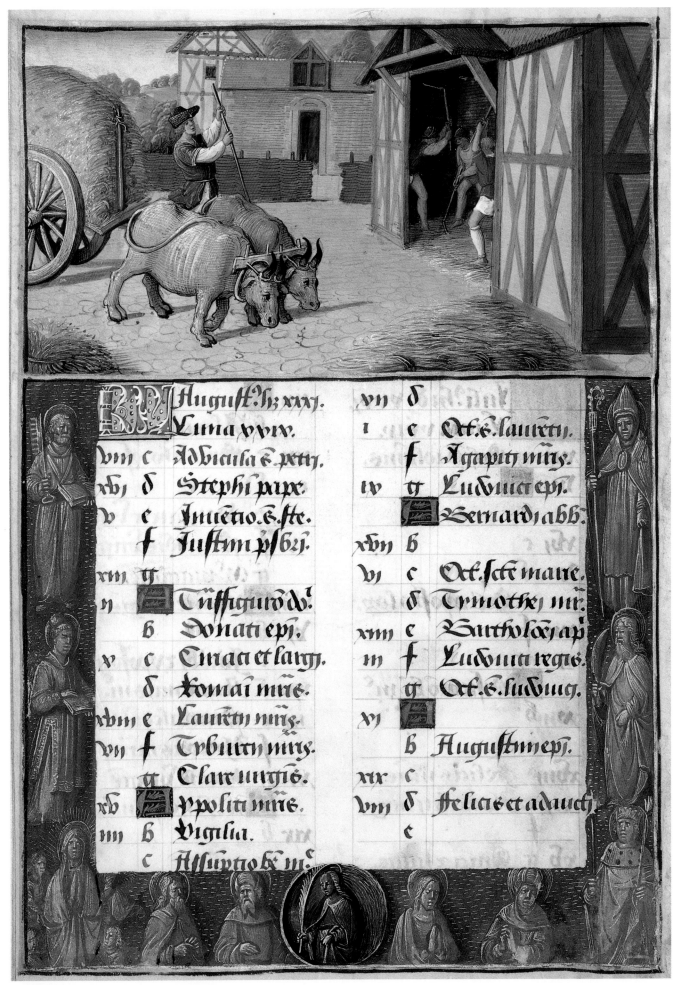

August: Threshing (fol. 4v)

The wheat harvest continues in August. The cut stalks are brought in ox carts to the barn where three men beat them with jointed flails. Threshing with flails loosens the kernels of wheat from their stalks so that they can then be winnowed and thus separated from the chaff.

In the left margin are Sts. Peter (for the Feast of St. Peter in Chains, August 1), Stephen, with a rock on his head (for the feast of the discovery of his relics, August 3), and the Assumption of the Virgin (August 15). The two male saints without attributes probably represent in a general way the martyrs listed in the first half of the month: Cyriac and Largus (August 8), Romanus (August 9), Tiburtius (August 11), or Hippolytus (August 13). At the right are Sts. Louis of Toulouse (August 19) or possibly Bernard of Clairvaux (August 20), Bartholomew the Apostle, holding his butcher's knife (August 24), and King Louis IX of France (August 25). The two women without attributes probably represent female saints in general, since there is only one female saint, Clare (August 12), listed in the month other than the Virgin. The zodiacal sign is Virgo, the Virgin (holding a palm of martyrdom).

September: Treading Grapes (fol. 5)

The labor for September is wine making. In the fields in the left background, seated women pick the grapes. When their baskets are full, men carry them to the barn and empty them into large winepresses where the fruit is trampled. Crushed, the grapes are then transferred to a large vat from which, at the bottom, the liquid can be extracted for storing and aging in the nearby barrels.

In the left margin are Sts. Giles, petting a hind (September 1), Anne, shown holding the Virgin (for the Feast of the Birth of the Virgin, September 8), the True Cross (for the Feast of the Exaltation of the Cross, September 14), Matthew the Apostle (September 21), and possibly St. Euphemia (September 16). In the right margin are Sts. Maurice and his companions (September 22), Michael the Archangel, shown slaying a demon (his feast on September 29, however, is not entered in the Calendar), and Cosmas and Damian (September 27). The zodiacal sign is Libra, the Balance.

Septeber h3 vvv.
Luna xxix.

vbi f Egidii abbis.
v g Antonini mr̃
[ ] A
vm b
n c
d
v e
f Nat. b̃. m̃
xbm g Gorgonii mr̃s.
vn E Nicolai conf.
b Prothi mr̃s.
xb c
m d
e Eustacio̅ s̃ auc.
vm f Oct. beate marie.

Eusenne virgie
A
w b
vbm d Vigilia.
vi e Matĥi ap̃.
f Maurici eu s ep.
vim g Lini p̃r z mr̃s
m A
b
vi c Cypriani mr̃s.
xix d Cosme mr̃s.
e
vm f
g Jeronimi pbr̃i.
[ ] A

October

October: Sowing and Ploughing (fol. 5v)

In October the winter wheat is sown. The man on the right plows his field with a team of white horses. The man at left sows the field with grain from his apron.

In the left margin are Sts. Remigius (October 1) and Francis, receiving the stigmata (October 4). They are followed by two bishop saints of whom one is undoubtedly Cerbonius (October 10), and Pope Calixtus (October 14). The right margin begins with a bishop saint without attribute followed by Luke the Evangelist (October 18). He is followed by the Apostle Simon, holding a club (his Feast, with Jude's, on October 28) and Ivo (his translation, on October 27), shown in discussion with the Apostle Jude (October 28). The zodiacal sign is Scorpio, the Scorpion.

November: Thrashing for Acorns (fol. 6)

In November the labor is to take the pigs to the forest, rattle the branches of the oak trees so they shed their acorns, and thus fatten the animals up.

In the left margin are a large group of saints (for the Feast of All Saints, November 1), Death as a skeleton (for the feast of All Souls, November 2), and Sts. Martin (bishop of Tours, November 11) and Brictius (archbishop of Tours, November 13). At the right are Sts. Catherine, with a palm of martyrdom and the sword of her decapitation (November 25), Andrew the Apostle, holding his X-shaped cross (November 30), Clement, in papal tiara (November 23), and Cecilia (November 22). The zodiacal sign is Sagittarius, the Archer.

December: Roasting Slaughtered Pigs (fol. 6v)

In December, the pigs that were fattened in November are killed. At the right a woman has collected their blood in a large pan. Resting on a bed of kindling and covered with twigs, the hogs are singed prior to butchering, for which the man prepares by sharpening his knife.

The left margin shows the Meeting of Joachim and Anne at the Golden Gate (for the Feast of the Conception of the Virgin, December 8), Sts. Barbara, holding her tower (December 4), and Nicholas, shown resuscitating the three pickled youths (December 6). At the right are St. Thomas the Apostle, holding a builder's square (December 21), the Nativity (December 25), Sts. Stephen Protomartyr, with a rock on his head (December 26), John the Evangelist, blessing a cup of poison (December 27), and a group of the Holy Innocents (December 28). The zodiacal sign is Capricorn, the Goat.

GOSPEL LESSONS

(fols. 7–21v)

By the beginning of the fifteenth century, four particular Gospel Lessons had become a regular feature in Books of Hours. These Lessons, which often follow the Calendar, are actually the Gospel readings from the Masses for four of the Church's major liturgical feasts. These holy days are Christmas (December 25; the reading is taken from the third, or main, Mass of the day), the Feast of the Annunciation (March 25), Epiphany (January 6), and Ascension (a movable feast whose date depended upon that of Easter). Because they were read as part of the Mass, these Lessons can thus be found in the Missal, the service book used by the priest at Mass. This overlap between Missal and Book of Hours was, of course, a great attraction for the *Horae* user. Reading these biblical passages in their Books of Hours, laymen and laywomen knew they were praying the identical texts from the Church's official liturgy. With these passages, they also knew they were reading the literal Word of God, which they possessed only in their Books of Hours because, during this period, laypeople did not own or read from Bibles.

The first Gospel Lesson, from John (1:1–14), acts as a kind of preamble for the entire Book of Hours. Its theme is humankind's need of redemption and God's willingness to provide it. Opening with the famous passage, *"In principio erat verbum"* (In the beginning was the Word), the Lesson starts with the theme of Christ's Divinity and then discusses the witness of John the Baptist, the Jews' rejection of Christ, Christians as the new children of God, and ends with the Incarnation. The Gospel Lesson of Luke (1:26–38) describes the Annunciation and ends with the Virgin's acceptance of God's will. The Lesson from Matthew (2:1–12) tells the story of the Three Magi, their journey and interview with Herod, their worship of Christ and gifts to him, and, finally, their return home. The Lesson of Mark (16:14–20) relates Christ's appearances to the apostles after his Resurrection and ends with his Ascension.

The alert reader will have noticed that Christ's Passion—one of the most important events of the Savior's life—is not covered by the four Gospel Lessons just discussed. This lacuna was clearly felt in the late Middle Ages, and beginning in the early fifteenth century, the Passion according to John (18:1–19:42) began to appear in Books of Hours. By the end of the century it became a nearly standard feature (especially in printed *Horae*), where it constituted a fifth Lesson, often, as here, following the other four. John's is the haunting eyewitness account by the one apostle who, along with Mary, remained at the foot of the Cross during the entire Crucifixion. It was his version of the Passion with which medieval men and women would have been most familiar, as it was read or chanted on Good Friday. On this day, medieval Christians imitated the evangelist's devotion in a service where they would join in procession, kneel, and kiss a statue of Christ crucified (called "creeping to the cross" in England).

—R.S.W.

John's Lesson: John on Patmos
border: John Boiled in Oil (fol. 7)

Luke's Lesson: Luke Writing
border: Annunciation (fol. 9)

Matthew's Lesson: Matthew Writing
border: Magi Meeting at the Crossroads (fol. 10v)

Mark's Lesson: Mark Contemplating
border: Christ Preaching to a Crowd (fol. 12)

Typically, as here, the Gospel Lessons are illustrated with a cycle of evangelist portraits, one placed at the beginning of each reading. Thus the miniatures in the Hours of Henry VIII follow a tradition from classical antiquity (and kept alive in the Middle Ages) of placing an author portrait at the beginning of his text. These four miniatures follow the iconography conventional for Books of Hours by showing Luke, Matthew, and Mark seated in their studies, writing their texts in bound codices. (Were they to be depicted writing on loose, unbound sheets—as was the actual practice in the Middle Ages and Renaissance—the evangelists would have looked more like scribes and less like authors.) John, who writes on a scroll, does so on Patmos, the island to which he was banished by the Roman emperor Domitian (r. 81–96) and where, according to tradition, he wrote the Book of Revelation. As was customary, each evangelist is accompanied by his symbol: an eagle for John, an ox for Luke, an angel for Matthew, and a lion for Mark.

In addition to author portraits, Gospel Lessons were sometimes illustrated with episodes from the life of the evangelist or, more rarely, events

described in the texts themselves. The Hours of Henry VIII combines all of these traditions. The border of the first Lesson illustrates the scene of John Boiled in Oil. Before banishing him to Patmos, the emperor Domitian had tried to rid himself of the evangelist by boiling him to death. In the border, one man heats up the fire with bellows to such a temperature that his colleagues must shield their faces from the blast. John, calmly praying in the tub, remains unharmed.

For the next three Lessons, events mentioned in the opening words of the text are illustrated in the borders. Luke's text opens, *"In illo tempore. Missus est Gabriel angelus a D[e]o in civitatem Galilee cui nomen Nazareth"* (In that time, the angel Gabriel was sent from God to a town of Galilee called Nazareth). God the Father is given a prominent role in this Annunciation, directing both Gabriel and the Dove of the Holy Spirit toward the Virgin Annunciate. Matthew's Lesson begins, *"Cum natus esset Ihesus in Bethleem Iude in diebus Herodis regis, ecce Magi ab Oriente venerunt Ierosolimam"* (When Jesus was born in Bethlehem of Judea, in the days of King Herod, behold, Magi came from the East to Jerusalem). The border shows the Three Kings, accompanied by their entourages, meeting at the crossroads en route to where the star leads them. The fourth Gospel Lesson, that of Mark, opens, *"In illo tempore. Recumbe[n]tibus undecim discipulis apparuit illis Ih[es]us"* (In that time, Jesus appeared to the eleven disciples). Christ's stern gesture, leveled at the group, reflects his upbraiding the apostles for their lack of faith and hardness of heart.

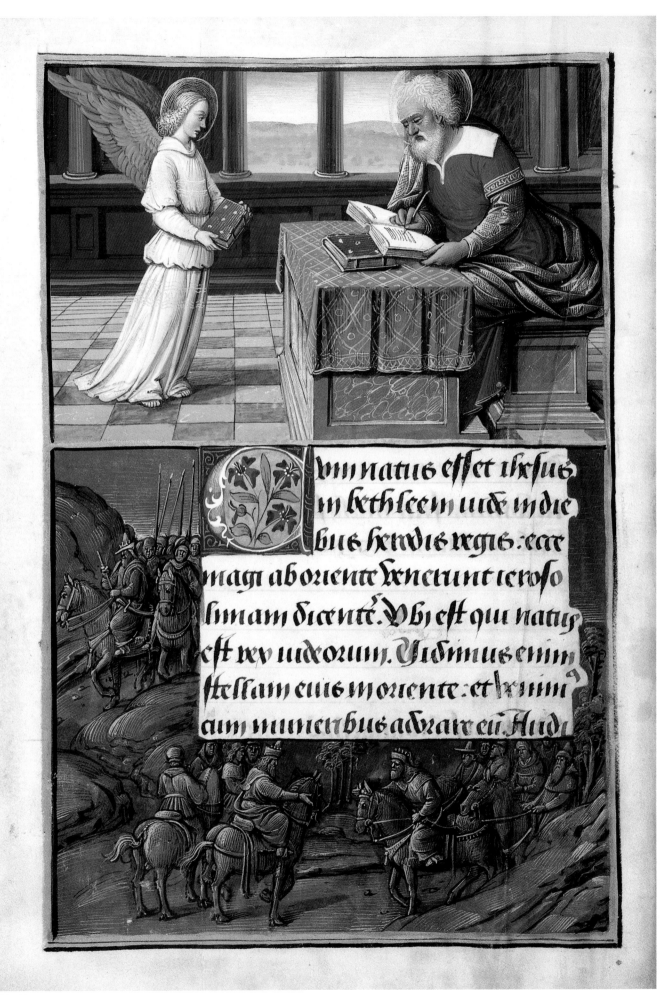

um natus esset ihesus
in bethleem iude in die
bus herodis regis: ecce
magi ab oriente venerunt ieroso
limam dicente. Vbi est qui natus
est rex iudeorum. Uidimus enim
stellam eius in oriente: et venimus
cum muneribus adorare eu. Aud[

N illo tempore: Recumbe
tibus vndecim discipulis
apparuit illis ihüs: et ex
probrauit incredulitatem illorū
et durciam cordis: quia his viđ
rant cum resurrexisse non credide
rant. Et dixit eis. Euntes i mun
dum vniuersum predicate euange

Passion according to John: "Ego sum" (fol. 13)

John's Passion is normally illustrated with an image of Christ's Agony in the Garden or, as here, of the *"Ego sum"* (I am he). As an incident only related by John, the *"Ego sum"* is the more iconographically appropriate of the two subjects. The Latin title of the picture derives from the short but dramatic answer Christ gave to the rough band of soldiers who had come with Judas to arrest him; at his two words (as seen in the miniature), the crowd fell back in amazement. Behind Christ, St. Peter begins to draw his sword, while other disciples turn to flee in terror. Within the group of soldiers on the ground Judas can be identified as the bearded figure at the left clutching his moneybag. The miniature is painted as if it were a small framed panel. At the top is the rubric, *"Passio Domini Nostri Iesu Christi s[e]cumdum* [sic: *secundum] Iohannem"* (The Passion of Our Lord Jesus Christ according to John). At the bottom are the opening words of the text itself, *"Egr[e]ssus est D[omi]n[u]s Iesu cu[m] discipulis suis tra[n]s torrente[m] Cedro[n]"* (Our Lord Jesus Christ went forth with his disciples over the brook Cedron).

The iconography of Poyet's nighttime scene can ultimately be traced back to the version painted by the Limbourg brothers in Jean, duc de Berry's *Très Riches Heures* (shortly before 1416), a miniature that, like many in his famous manuscript, was highly influential for French illumination.

EGRSSUS EST DNS IESUS CU DISCIPULIS SUIS TRAS TORRETE CEDRO

Prayers to the Virgin

(fols. 21v – 29v)

In addition to the more or less standard texts found in Books of Hours—Calendar, Gospel Lessons, Hours of the Virgin, Hours of the Cross, Hours of the Holy Spirit, Penitential Psalms with Litany, Office of the Dead, and Suffrages—almost innumerable accessory prayers also make their appearance. From both their frequency and their variety, it is clear that these added devotions were eagerly included by owners who wanted to personalize their prayer books. The Hours of Henry VIII contains a number of these "extra" prayers. They include the set of four Marian devotions that follow the Gospel Lessons—the *"Obsecro te,"* *"O intemerata,"* *"Stabat mater,"* and Mass of the Virgin—plus the devotion called the Seven Prayers of St. Gregory, and, at the very end, an unillustrated series of practical prayers for everyday use (briefly discussed in chapter 1 and listed in appendix A).

Of all the optional prayers that owners requested, by far the most popular were two to the Virgin called, after their Latin *incipits* (opening words), the *"Obsecro te"* (I beseech you) and the *"O intemerata"* (O incomparable one). In the *"Obsecro te"* the reader addresses the Virgin directly, in plaintive tones and in the first person singular. "I beseech you, Mary," the prayer begins, "holy lady, mother of God, most full of piety, daughter of the greatest king, most glorious mother, mother of orphans, consolation of the desolate, the way for those who stray, salvation for those who hope in you," and continues by asking the Virgin's assistance in securing mercy from her Son. The prayer ends by asking the Virgin to reveal the penitent reader's day and hour of death.

The end of the *"Obsecro te"* and the beginning of the *"O intemerata"* are both missing from the manuscript; these were on a leaf that is lacking between the present folios 23 and 24. The leaf was probably excised because of its miniature marking the beginning of the *"O intemerata."* Like the previous prayer, this one is also written in the first person singular and appeals to the Virgin as intercessor in her special role as a faithful mother at her Son's death.

The emotional intensity, rhythm, and rhymes of the *"Stabat mater"* made this prayer extremely popular in Books of Hours. Its theme is the Virgin's compassionate fidelity to her Son during the Crucifixion:

> *Stabat mater dolorosa*
> *Juxta crucem lacri[m]osa*
> *Dum pendebat filius*
> *Cuius animam gementem*
> *Contristantem et dolentem*
> *Pertransivit gladius....*

> *At the Cross her station keeping*
> *Stood the mournful mother weeping*
> *Close to Jesus to the last*
> *Through her heart his sorrow sharing*
> *All his bitter anguish bearing*
> *Now at length the sword has passed....*

The Mass of the Virgin is the fourth devotion in this series of accessory Marian prayers between the Gospel Lessons and the Hours of the Virgin. Since the leaf that originally faced the beginning of the Mass on folio 28 is lacking (it also contained the last verses of the *"Stabat mater,"* which are missing), it most likely had a miniature.

—R.S.W.

per te ihu xpx saluator mundi.
Qui in trinitate perfecta vivis et
regnas deus per omnia secula se
culorum. amen. Et sic maria. oro.

Et ave domina scta
maria mater dei pie
tate plenissima sum
regis filia mater gloriosissima

fol. 21v

"Obsecro te": Holy Family
border: Musical Angels (fol. 21v)

Since the first part of the *"Obsecro te"* emphasizes the Virgin's special role in the Incarnation and reminds her of the joys of motherhood, miniatures illustrating the prayer, as in the Hours of Henry VIII, depict the Virgin with the Christ Child. Here St. Joseph, in an important parental role he is rarely given in Books of Hours, offers Jesus a pear. *"Obsecro te"* miniatures often include musical angels: here they serenade the Holy Family with a lute, pipe and tabor, portative organ, and trumpet marine.

"Stabat mater": Lamentation
border: Deposition (fol. 26)

The half-page miniature that marks the opening of the *"Stabat mater"* depicts the Lamentation. The Virgin, flanked by John the Evangelist and Mary Magdalene, holds the dead Christ on her lap. Behind them, on Golgotha, looms the empty Cross; the two thieves have yet to be taken down. The border illustrates the event that took place just before the Lamentation, the Deposition. The Virgin, again accompanied by John and the Magdalene, awaits the delivery of her dead Son's body by Nicodemus and Joseph of Arimathea.

E tabat mater dolorosa.
Iuxta crucem lacriosa.
Dum pendebat filius.
Cuius animam gementem.
Contristantem et dolentem.
Pertransiuit gladius.
Qui tristis et afflicti.
fuit illa benedicta.

HOURS OF THE VIRGIN

(fols. 31–93v)

The Hours of the Virgin are the core text of a Book of Hours and, as their title indicates, are devoted to Mary, the Mother of God. Their importance, moreover, is signaled in the Hours of Henry VIII both by length (some sixty folios) and the richness of their illumination, which includes more than half of the manuscript's full-page miniatures. These mark the beginnings of the first seven of the eight "Hours" that make up the text (the miniature for the eighth Hour is missing). These Hours, known as the canonical Hours, are patterned after the eight occurrences of daily prayer found in the Breviary. Matins, frequently combined with Lauds, was said at night or upon rising. Prime, the first Hour of the day in ancient Roman and thus medieval timekeeping, was recited at about 6:00 A.M. The next three Hours were recited at intervals of about three hours: Terce, the third Hour of the day (9:00 A.M.); Sext, the sixth Hour (around noon); and None, the ninth Hour (3:00 P.M.). Vespers was the evening office, and Compline, the last Hour, was said before retiring. Except for the first, Matins, which also has lessons, each round of prayer includes a selection of verses, responses, a hymn, antiphons, psalms, a capitulum, and prayers; many of these are addressed to the Virgin.

The beginning text of the first Hour, Matins, on folio 31, puts the devout in the proper frame of mind:

> **Versicle.** *Domine labia mea aperies*
> *(Lord, thou shalt open my lips).*
> **Response.** *Et os meum annuntiabit laudem tuam (And my mouth shall declare thy praise).*

The second versicle and response open the other hours (except Compline):

> **Versicle.** *Deus in adjutorium meum intende*
> *(O God, hasten to mine aid).*
> **Response.** *Domine, ad adjuvandum me festina (O Lord, make haste to help me).*

The subjects of the full-page miniatures form a chronological cycle dealing with important events in the early life of the Virgin—the Infancy of Christ—though the episodes are not, for the most part, specifically mentioned in their respective texts. Through repeated association with specific Hours, however, the images served as bookmarks as well as objects for meditation or devotion. The text for Sext, for example, which is introduced with a miniature depicting the Adoration of the Magi (see fol. 61v), makes no reference to that subject. Nevertheless, since it is one of the shorter hours, and includes the typical kinds of prayers found in the various hours, we have provided its text below.

> **Versicle.** *O God, hasten to mine aid.*
> **Response.** *O Lord, make haste to help me.*
> *Glory be to the Father, and to the Son, and to the Holy Ghost. As it was in the beginning, is now, and ever shall be, world with out end. Amen.*

> **Hymn.**
> *Remember, O Creator Lord,*
> *That in the Virgin's sacred womb*
> *Thou wast conceived, and of her flesh*
> *Didst our mortality assume.*
>
> *Mother of Grace! O Mary blest!*
> *To thee, sweet fount of life, we fly;*
> *Shield us through life, and take us hence,*
> *To thy dear bosom, when we die.*
>
> *O Jesu! born of Virgin bright,*
> *Immortal glory be to Thee,*

Praise to the Father infinite,
  And Holy Ghost eternally. Amen.

Antiphon. *We run after the sweet smell of thine ointments: maidens have loved thee exceedingly.*

Psalm 122. *To thee have I lifted up my eyes. . . . Glory be, etc.*

Psalm 123. *If it had not been. . . . Glory be, etc.*

Psalm 124. *They that trust in the Lord. . . . Glory be, etc.*

Antiphon. *We run after the sweet smell of thine ointments: maidens have loved thee exceedingly.*

Capitulum. *And I took root in an honorable people, and in the portion of my God, his inheritance: and my abode is in the full assembly of saints.* (Ecclesiasticus 24:16)

Versicle. *Blessed art thou amongst women.*

Response.
  And blessed is the fruit of thy womb.
  Lord, have mercy on us.

Christ, have mercy on us.
  Lord, have mercy on us.

Versicle. *O Lord, hear my prayer.*

Response. *And let my cry come unto Thee.*

Prayer. *O most merciful God, grant succor unto our frailty; that as we celebrate the memory of the holy Mother of God, so by the help of her intercession we may rise again from our transgressions. Through the same Jesus Christ, thy Son, Our Lord, who liveth and reigneth with thee in the unity of the Holy Spirit, God, world without end.*

The cycle of miniatures is fairly standard, starting with the Annunciation and ending with the Massacre of the Innocents; the emphasis is clearly on the Incarnation and Infancy of Christ. The eighth miniature, for Compline, is missing, but probably depicted the Coronation of the Virgin, her reward in heaven.

—W.M.V.

93

Matins: Annunciation (fol. 30v)

The traditional opening miniature in most Hours of the Virgin is, as here, the Annunciation. This is not surprising since the recitation of every Hour is preceded by the prayer known as the Hail Mary, whose opening words also form the Invitatory on the facing text page, which can easily be found after the rubric, *"Invitator[ium]. Ave maria gratia plena dominus tecum"* (Hail, Mary, full of grace, the Lord is with thee). These are, of course, the very words with which Archangel Gabriel addressed the Virgin at the Annunciation (Luke 1:28). When told that she would conceive and bring forth a son who was to be named Jesus, the Virgin was perplexed, as she knew no man. Gabriel replied that the Holy Spirit would come upon her and that the power of the Most High would overshadow her.

In the miniature we are about to witness the Incarnation of Christ, when the eternal Son of God took human flesh from his human mother. God the Father, in a flaming aureole supported by a choir of red angels, dispatches the Holy Spirit in the form of a dove, who follows a path of golden rays toward the Virgin. While Poyet may have intended the red angels to be seraphim, the highest order of angels and those closest to God, he has given them full bodies and one rather than three pairs of wings. Mary, who stands rather than kneels, has her eyes turned downward on an open book in a red chemise binding supported by a green cushion. In Annunciations from the late Middle Ages, these books take on the shape of a Book of Hours. Indeed, the manuscript shown here, in size and layout, is much like the Hours of Henry VIII. Gabriel, on one knee, holds a scepter surmounted with a fleur-de-lis and wears an alb and a blue stole ornamented with gold crosses, anticipating the priestly vestments worn at Mass and when handling the Blessed Sacrament. (The Eucharist was believed to be the real presence of the Body and Blood of Christ, the human form assumed by God at the Incarnation.) The Annunciation takes place in an open portico, whose two arches frame and heighten the figures, while diagonals and orthogonals lead the eye into the garden and distant city, offering testimony to Poyet's legendary skill in the use of perspective. The spatial clarity, indeed, seems classical in the Italian sense, and is not cluttered with unnecessary or fussy details (such as the customary lilies); it is further enhanced by the miniature's simple frame and the undecorated borders. This restraint applies to the facing text page as well, with its understated introductory initial and small text box (which is smaller than the full-page miniature).

Domine labia mea aperies. Et os meum annunciabit laudem tuam. Deus in adiutorium meum intende. Domine ad adiuvandum me festina. Gloria patri et filio et spiritui sancto. Sicut erat in principio et nunc et semper: et in secula seculorum. Alleluia. Invitatorium. Ave maria gratia plena dominus tecum. Venite exultemus do. domino iubilemus deo salutari nostro: preoccupemus faciem

fol. 40v

Lauds: Visitation (fol. 40v)

According to Luke (1:36–56), Gabriel also told the Virgin that her cousin Elizabeth, in her old age, had also conceived a son. Soon thereafter, to rejoice, Mary went to visit her cousin, who was six months pregnant with John the Baptist. (Elizabeth was barren until Gabriel appeared to Zacharias, her husband, telling him that his wife would bear him a son that he should name John.) When the Virgin entered her house and greeted Elizabeth, the infant John leaped in her womb and she was filled with the Holy Spirit. Here, however, as is usual in art, the meeting takes place outdoors; the Virgin extends her hand to Elizabeth, who folds her hands in prayerful recognition of the forthcoming Savior. The burlet on Elizabeth's head, as well as the two purses hanging from her elaborate gold belt, give her an exotic appearance. The tired man standing behind the pair—his eyes half shut—is Joseph.

Prime: Nativity (fol. 51v)

Of the four evangelists, only Luke (2:7) provides details, though scant, concerning the Nativity: "And she brought forth her firstborn son, and wrapped him in swaddling clothes, and laid him in a manger, because there was no room for them in the inn." Here, however, the child is shown naked, revealing his maleness, and golden rays emanate from his body. These details derive from the Revelations of St. Bridget of Sweden (c. 1303–1373), which influenced depictions of the Nativity in the fifteenth and sixteenth centuries. According to Bridget, an ineffable light and splendor radiated from the child. Further, she continued, the shepherds—three are peering from the background—uninformed whether the child was male or female, wished to confirm that the child was indeed male; they knew that the Messiah should be a son. The presence of the ox and ass, not mentioned by the Gospels, but included by Bridget, had already been exegetically connected with the Nativity because they were thought to fulfill the prophecy of Isaiah (1:3), that the "ox knoweth his owner, and the ass his master's crib." Sometimes, as here, the animals are not equal witnesses but represent the contrast between the Old and New Dispensation, or the Old and New Law. The ox, symbolizing the New Law (of Christ) knowingly looks on, while the view of the other, the Old Law (of Moses), is obscured, and thus uncomprehending. After the birth, said Bridget, the Virgin immediately worshiped the child, as did Joseph.

The partially obscured object in the lower left corner is the saddle upon which Mary rode during her trip to Bethlehem, where the prophets said that the Messiah would be born.

Terce: Annunciation to the Shepherds (fol. 56v)

The Annunciation to the Shepherds, like the Nativity, is only recounted by
Luke (2:8–14). Poyet, however, has not chosen to emphasize the nocturnal
appearance of the single annunciatory angel amid the brightness of God, but
the later moment when the angel, joined by others from the heavenly hosts,
sang the familiar "Glory to God in the Highest, and on earth peace to men
of good will," the words on their scroll *("Gloria in exelssi* [sic: *excelsis] Deo et
in terra pax").* Three shepherds in the foreground, seen from the back or side,
look up and receive the tidings. One holds a staff while another with a bag-
pipe has a second instrument—a flute—tucked into his belt; the shep-
herdess holds a distaff. One wonders if the solitary and prominently placed
goat among the sheep in the middle would have recalled Matthew 25:32,
where the future Son of Man would come to judge and separate the blessed
from the evil, "just as the shepherd separates the sheep from the goats."
Wooden sheds in the background contain more sheep and two shepherds,
who are not yet aware of what has taken place in the foreground.

Sext: Adoration of the Magi (fol. 61v)

According to the Gospel of Matthew (2:1–12), wise men from the East who saw the star signifying the birth of the King of the Jews went to adore him at Jerusalem, only to discover that he was born in Bethlehem (fulfilling the prophecy of Micheas 5:2). Since the wise men offered three gifts—gold, frankincense, and myrrh—it was assumed as early as the third century that they were three; about the same time they were redefined as kings, and by the ninth century they were supplied with the familiar names of Caspar (the oldest), Balthazar, and Melchior (the youngest). In the later Middle Ages, when the Magi were connected with the three then known continents (Europe, Africa, Asia), Balthazar was increasingly depicted as a black man. In some late fifteenth-century paintings, however, as here, it was the youngest Magus who was so depicted. Their gifts were also given various explanations. According to St. Bernard of Clairvaux (1090–1153), the gold gave testimony to the Virgin's poverty, the incense purified the smell of the stable, and myrrh strengthened the child's limbs (driving out the worms from his entrails). For the Venerable Bede (672/73–735) they signified the royalty, divinity, and humanity of Christ: gold for royal tribute to the highest king; incense for divine worship since he was God; and myrrh for burial, foreshadowing his own death, since he was a mortal man. These explanations were popularized in printed editions of the *Golden Legend* (compiled by Jacobus de Voragine before 1267).

In Poyet's Adoration, the Virgin, in an act of humility, sits on the ground as each of the Magi presents his gift to the child standing on her lap. The oldest Magus, who has removed his crown in deference to Christ as King, kneels and presents gold; the second, holding a chalice with incense, waits his turn; while the youngest, still at a distance, stands erect and holds a monstrance. The innate nobility of the last is achieved by some of Poyet's most inspired painting, especially evident in his closely observed facial features, gold earring, and exotic turban. The same cannot be said for the rather weak "star that stood over the place where the Child was." In any case, Poyet designs his compositions like stage sets: the ruinous stone arches of the stable will reappear in the Massacre of the Innocents (see fol. 69v), and the ox and ass eat hay from the wattled manger that previously served as Christ's cradle.

None: Presentation in the Temple (fol. 65v)

The traditional illustration for None is the Presentation of Christ in the Temple, of which the only biblical account is Luke's (2:22–40): "After the days of her purification . . . they carried him to Jerusalem, to present him to the Lord . . . as it is written that every male opening the womb shall be called holy to the Lord, and to offer a sacrifice . . . a pair of turtledoves or two young pigeons." (The sacrificial birds were, following Leviticus 12:6–8, for the purification of women after childbirth.) Further, according to Luke, the Holy Family would be met by Simeon, who was inspired by the Holy Spirit to recognize, before his own death, the Savior. As was common in later medieval art, Poyet has identified Simeon with the high priest of the Temple; he would proclaim that the Lord could now let him depart in peace, having seen his salvation. The famous Canticle of Simeon, beginning *"Nunc dimittis"* (Now you may dismiss me), does occur in the Hours of the Virgin, but at Compline! Poyet has given him a halo because he was subsequently made a saint; the letters on the hem of his garment suggest Hebrew. After blessing the Holy Family, Simeon told Mary that her child was set for the fall and resurrection of many in Israel and that a sword would pierce her own soul. The five large crosses that decorate the altar cloth, suggesting the five wounds Christ would endure on the Cross, may allude to Simeon's prophecy.

The unusual presence of a Franciscan friar behind the altar suggests that the original owner may have had some connection or special devotion to that order, which was especially favored by French royalty at this time. The manuscript's Calendar (as is noted in appendix A) has a strong emphasis on Franciscans. They were known as Gray Friars because of the color of their habit, which was originally gray (but later brown). The altar itself, complete with a blue canopy and red curtains, is situated within a Renaissance interior with walls decorated with pilasters framing large red and green marble panels, echoing the rows of colored floor marbles.

Vespers: Massacre of the Innocents and Flight into Egypt
(fol. 69v)

Matthew, following his unique account of the Adoration of the Magi, continues the narrative (2:13–18) with the Flight into Egypt and the Massacre of the Innocents. Herod, learning that a future ruler of Israel would come from Bethlehem, ordered the killing of all male children two years old and younger living in or near Bethlehem. An angel had already appeared to Joseph in his sleep, telling him to take Jesus and his mother to Egypt until the death of Herod.

While the Massacre of the Innocents is less common than the Flight into Egypt as the Vesper illustration, Poyet managed to include both. As the slaughter takes place in the foreground, the Holy Family departs for Egypt in the background—as can be seen through the stone ruins. (Biblical scholars, indeed Matthew himself, have recognized that the Massacre and Flight provided the pretext for the fulfillment of Hosea's prophecy [Hosea 11:1] that, like Moses, the Messiah would come up out of Egypt.) At the right two mothers futilely attempt to keep their children from soldiers, while a woman on the left uncontrollably wails over her dead baby. The Holy Innocents were regarded as the first martyrs, and their feast day (three days after Christmas) was already celebrated by the early Church.

HOURS OF THE CROSS *(fols. 95–101)*
AND HOURS OF THE HOLY SPIRIT *(fols. 102–106v)*

Since the Hours of the Virgin stress her role in the Incarnation and their cycle of miniatures traditionally illustrates the Infancy of Christ, it is not surprising that the Hours of the Cross, which emphasizes his Passion, should frequently, as here, come next. The Hours of the Holy Spirit, on the other hand, are almost always paired with and proceed from the Hours of the Cross, just as Christ promised the apostles at the Last Supper that the Father would later send the Holy Spirit to teach them all things (John 14:26) and that the latter's power would come upon them (Acts 1:4).

The two Hours are much shorter than the Hours of the Virgin and follow the same sequence, except that there is no Lauds. Each Hour consists of two pairs of versicles and responses, a *"Gloria Patri"* followed by an antiphon, a short hymn with a versicle and response, and a prayer (there are no lengthy psalms). The opening versicles and responses are identical to those in the corresponding Hours of the Virgin, beginning with the familiar *"Domine labia mea aperies"* (Lord, thou shalt open my lips). Unlike the Hours of the Virgin, however, the different hymns for each Hour of the Cross form a chronological meditation on the Passion of Christ. The Matins hymn, for example, treats his Betrayal and Arrest. It begins with the words *"Patris sapiencia"* on folio 95:

Circled by his enemies,
By his own forsaken,
Christ the Lord at Matin Hour
For our sakes was taken:
Very Wisdom, Very Light,
Monarch long expected,
In the garden by the Jews
Bound, reviled, rejected.

The following hymns, in turn, deal with Christ before Pilate (Prime), his Crowning with Thorns (Terce), Crucifixion (Sext), death (None), Deposition (Vespers), Entombment (Compline), and an invocation for Christ's comfort at the time of the reader's death. Each of the hymns originally formed an eight-part poem, perhaps composed in the twelfth century, which connected Christ's Passion with the canonical Hours.

As with the Hours of the Cross, the hymns for each of the separate Hours of the Holy Spirit were also taken from a poem *("Nobis sancti Spiritus")*, the eight parts of which are thematically related to the Holy Spirit: the Incarnation (Matins), redemption through Christ's Passion (Prime), Pentecost (Terce), proselytization by the apostles (Sext), qualities of the Holy Spirit (None), the Holy Spirit as protector (Vespers), the Last Judgment (Compline), and a stanza asking the Holy Spirit for aid in achieving eternal salvation in heaven.

Since the standard illustration for the Hours of the Holy Spirit is Pentecost, an event that the *Golden Legend* placed at the Hour of Terce, we have translated the Terce hymn here:

God his Holy Spirit sent to his apostles dear,
On the day of Pentecost to yield them
    gladsome cheer,
And with fiery tongues in them did ardent
    zeal impress:
By no means could he endure to leave them
    comfortless.

—W.M.V.

111

fol. 94v

Hours of the Cross: Christ Carrying the Cross (fol. 94v)

Although it is usually the Crucifixion rather than the Carrying of the Cross that marks the beginning of the Hours of the Cross, the latter is sometimes, though more rarely, encountered. Examples date mostly toward the end of the fifteenth and early sixteenth centuries, when the *Imitation of Christ* became increasingly better known and widespread. The devotional treatise is usually ascribed to Thomas à Kempis (1379/80–1471) and may have been written about 1413, when he was ordained at age thirty-three. Indeed, the twelfth and last chapter of its second book has the title, "On the Royal Road of the Holy Cross." The basic theme derives from the words Jesus spoke to his disciples (Matthew 16:24): "If any man will come after me, let him deny himself, and take up his cross, and follow me." Thomas's chapter, in fact, begins with part of the quotation itself.

In the miniature, as in Poyet's triptych of 1485 in the Château of Loches (see fig. 16), Christ, slightly bent by the weight of the Cross, looks out at and gently draws the beholder to him. In the miniature he is still wearing the purple robe that was placed on him when he was mocked as the King of the Jews. Reflecting a later pictorial tradition (already seen in the late sixth-century Gospels of St. Augustine in Cambridge, Corpus Christi College, cod. 286, fol. 125), Christ is assisted by Simon of Cyrene. The third ingredient, the agonizing pair of the Virgin and John (not mentioned in the biblical texts), is a prominent feature of later meditational literature that emphasized their compassion. Passion plays and the Stations of the Cross, which were encouraged by the Franciscans and became popular at the end of the fifteenth century, also contributed to the iconography.

Hours of the Holy Spirit: Pentecost (fol. 101v)

Pentecost, or the Descent of the Holy Spirit, as described in the Acts of the Apostles (2:1–4), took place in a house where the disciples met on the Jewish feast of Pentecost. After a sound like a mighty wind came from heaven there appeared to them "parted tongues as it were of fire, and it sat upon every one of them." They were all filled with the Holy Spirit, and were given the ability to speak in diverse tongues. Poyet, in a well-established tradition, depicts the power of the Holy Spirit as golden rays emanating from a dove, symbol of the Holy Spirit. The dove, which has a cruciform halo, is directly above the Virgin, who is often included in the scene, though her presence is not specifically mentioned in the Acts. Such writers as St. Odilo of Cluny (c. 962–1049) simply assumed her presence; linking Pentecost with the earlier descent of the Holy Spirit that brought about the Incarnation, he argued that it would have been impossible to exclude her. The Virgin is surrounded by apostles, who are again twelve in number, Judas having been replaced by Matthias. The two apostles in the foreground are the youthful John (left) and Peter.

In the Middle Ages, the Christian feast of Pentecost (from the Greek word meaning "fiftieth day") was celebrated on the fiftieth day after Easter, just as the Jewish Pentecost was celebrated fifty days after Passover. As Easter is analogous to the Jewish Passover, there was a correspondence made between the two Pentecosts. The Jewish Pentecost commemorated Moses' reception of the Law, while the Christian feast instituted the Church and thus the New Law. The analogy was made, for example, in the *Biblia pauperum* (a late medieval typological treatise), where the two events were paired; according to the accompanying text, "Just as the law was given to Moses and was written on tables of stone, so, on the day of Pentecost, a new law was written in the hearts of the faithful collected together when the fire appeared above them."

PENITENTIAL PSALMS AND LITANY

(fols. 107v–127)

The Penitential Psalms and Litany generally follow, as here, the Hours of the Cross and the Hours of the Holy Spirit. According to medieval tradition the Seven Penitential Psalms were written by King David as penance for his grievous sins. In any case, the seven Psalms (6, 31, 37, 50, 101, 129, and 142) were long associated with atonement and had already formed a part of Jewish liturgy; they were certainly known by Christians in the West by the sixth century when Cassiodorus, a Roman historian, statesman, and monk, regarded them as a sevenfold means of obtaining forgiveness. Pope Innocent III (r. 1198–1216) ordered them to be recited during Lent, and, as a group, they were attached to the Breviary and the Book of Hours, where they were followed by the Litany and Office of the Dead (as in the present manuscript). The number of the Psalms eventually led them to be connected with the Seven Deadly Sins (pride, envy, anger, avarice, gluttony, sloth, and lust), with the result that they could be recited either as penance for having committed them or as a protection against them.

The first Penitential Psalm (6), which begins with the letter *D* on folio 109 *("Domine ne in furore tuo arguas me ne[que] in ira tua corripias me . . . ")* can be translated (in excerpts) as follows:

O Lord, rebuke me not in thy indignation, nor chastise me in thy wrath. Have mercy on me, O Lord, for I am weak: help me, O Lord, for my bones are troubled. And my soul is troubled exceedingly. . . . Turn to me, O Lord, and deliver my soul. . . . I will water my couch with my tears. . . . Depart from me, all ye workers of iniquity . . . for the Lord hath heard my supplication . . . my prayer. . . .

Whereas this psalm and the six others invoke the aid of the Lord, the Litany that immediately follows invokes the aid of a considerable number of saints who are asked to pray for the person reciting it. After an abbreviated *"Kyrie"* (a brief prayer for mercy), a celestial hierarchy of saints is named, beginning with the Three Persons of the Trinity, the Virgin Mary, archangels and other angels, and John the Baptist (our future intercessor at the Last Judgment); these are followed by apostles, male martyrs, confessors (male nonmartyr saints), female virgin martyrs, widows, and, finally, All Saints. To these are added various petitions against, among other calamities, lightning, earthquakes, plagues, and wars; petitions for deliverance in the name of events in Christ's life; other requests for help and consideration; and ending with various prayers for the dead. The text of the Litany usually continues, without a break, after the Penitential Psalms and is thus, as here, unillustrated.

—W.M.V.

David and Uriah (fol. 108v)

Although King David in Penance is the usual and obvious subject selected to mark the Penitential Psalms, his adultery with Bathsheba is also popular at this time. Somewhat rarer is the episode selected here, which occurred after his adultery, when he summoned to Jerusalem Uriah, her husband, who had conveniently been away serving in the army under Joab. To solve the problem of Bathsheba's pregnancy, the king sent a letter to Joab ordering him to place Uriah in the front of the battle, where he would surely be killed (2 Samuel 11:14–15). In the miniature, Bathsheba's husband, one knee deferentially bent, has already received the sealed order from David, while his ready white horse waits in the background. A shadowy figure stands by the canopied bed to the left, where the sin was consummated.

This theme was probably selected to introduce the first Penitential Psalm because David's order for Uriah's death was considered a sin of "anger." This Psalm is the only one to include the name of a specific Deadly Sin, *"ira"* (found on the fourth line of fol. 108), the Latin word for anger. In addition, the Penitential Psalms in some early sixteenth-century printed Parisian *Horae* are illustrated by the same subject, along with a rubric stating that the first Psalm should be invoked against that sin.

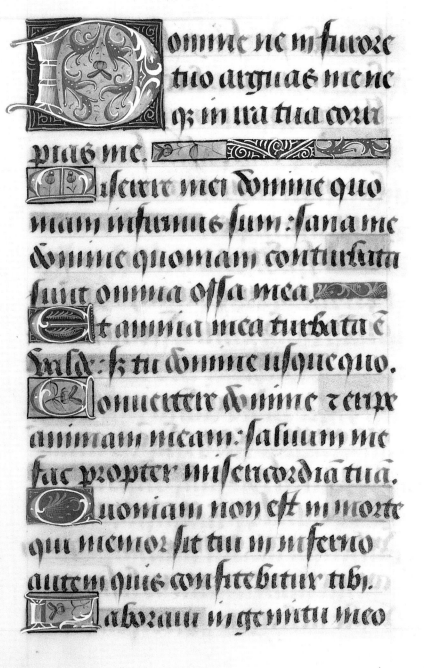

omine ne in furore
tuo arguas me ne
qz in ira tua corri
pias me. Miserere mei domine quo
niam infirmus sum: sana me
domine quoniam conturbata
sunt omnia ossa mea. Et anima mea turbata e
valde: sz tu domine usquequo.
Convertere domine et eripe
animam meam: saluum me
fac propter misericordiam tuam.
Quoniam non est in morte
qui memor sit tui in inferno
autem quis confitebitur tibi.
Laboraui in gemitu meo

OFFICE OF THE DEAD

(fols. 127–167v)

The Office of the Dead usually followed the Penitential Psalms and Litany, shifting the focus of prayer from oneself to the deceased, a function that was more clearly evident from its old name, the Office *for* the Dead. Its importance is indicated by its length (it is second only to the Hours of the Virgin) and by the fact that it is exactly the same Office as found in Breviaries and Antiphonaries. The threat of long periods of time in the painful fires of purgatory was a serious matter, and anything that could be done to shorten or alleviate such suffering for loved ones had to be considered. Even though the Bible suggested that God would render to every man according to his works (Psalm 61:13), the early Church Fathers had already affirmed that prayers for the dead helped loose them from sins. St. Thomas Aquinas (1225–1274), likewise, noted that charity extended not only to the living but also the dead, and that punishments in purgatory could be entirely done away by a multiplicity of prayers, adding that those praying for the dead reaped benefits as well. The Councils of Lyons I (1254) and Florence (1439) both asserted that purgatory was a place of expiation and that prayers for the dead were important. Such prayers could aid suffering souls for sins that remained unexpiated by penance at the time of death. Since those in purgatory cannot pray for themselves, said Aquinas, their condition requires that we pray for them.

The Office, the present form of which goes back to the early ninth century, consists only of three Hours: Vespers, Matins, and Lauds; these were also known as *"Placebo," "Dirige,"* and *"Exultabant,"* respectively, after the first words of their opening antiphons. The second, *"Dirige,"* gave rise to the present word *dirge,* referring to a mournful hymn at a funeral. Vespers was ideally prayed over the coffin in church on the evening before the funeral Mass. Monks were hired by the family to recite or chant it. Matins and Lauds were prayed, again by paid monks, on the morning of the funeral itself. The ordained, who recited the Office on a daily basis, provided an inspired model for the laity to pray it frequently at home. The purpose was the same, to help get the dearly departed out of purgatory as quickly as possible. As with most offices, each of the three Hours is composed of antiphons, psalms, versicles, and responses, except for Matins, which, as in the Hours of the Virgin, has three nocturns, each with three lessons. These psalms usually offer comfort to the dead; perhaps one of the most familiar is Psalm 22, the first recited in the second nocturn of Matins:

> *The Lord is my shepherd; I shall not want. He maketh me to lie down in green pastures: he leadeth me beside the still waters. He restoreth my soul: he leadeth me in the paths of righteousness for his name's sake. Yea, though I walk through the valley of the shadow of death, I will fear no evil. . . . "* (King James Version, where it is number 23)

The nine lessons are all taken from the Book of Job and are concerned with his pleadings for mercy and understanding. The extracts that follow, taken from several lessons, are typical:

> *How long wilt thou not spare me. . . . I have sinned, what shall I do to thee. . . . My soul is weary of life. . . . Do not condemn me: tell me why thou judgest me so? Make me know my crimes and offenses. . . . For thou writest bitter things against me, and consumest me for the sins of my youth. . . . Who will grant me this, that thou mayst protect me in hell. . . . Deliver me, O Lord, and set me beside thee. . . . For I know that my redeemer liveth, and on the last day I shall rise out of the earth. . . . And I shall be*

clothed again with my skin, and in my flesh I shall see my God.

The readings were selected in such a way that the name of Job is, in fact, never mentioned. Thus (as is clear from the extracts cited above), the first person singular pronoun, I, becomes the voice of the person reading the Office, undergoing trials and tribulations in his search for meaning, and for an understanding of and relationship to God. The Office ends with versicles and responses declaring the hoped for result.

    Versicle. *From the gates of Hell,*
    Response. *Deliver their souls, O Lord.*
    Versicle. *May they rest in peace.*
    Response. *Amen*

Although the Office of the Dead almost always contains a single miniature, the present manuscript has two. The second miniature, as here, usually marks the beginning of Matins, a division reflecting the practice of recitation observed above. Other examples are known, such as the Hours of Etienne Chevalier in Chantilly (Musée Condé, MS 71), which was painted by Jean Fouquet in the 1450s, and which Poyet had probably seen. Among the most common illustrations for the Office are various moments of the funeral (from deathbed to burial), the Last Judgment, Raising of Lazarus, personifications of Death, Job on the Dungheap, and the Parable of Dives and Lazarus. The last two subjects were selected here.

—W.M.V.

fol. 127v

Vespers: Job on the Dungheap (fol. 127v)

Although the nine Matins lessons are taken from the Book of Job, they do not specifically refer to the theme that frequently serves as a frontispiece for the Office, Job's discourse with his three friends, Eliphaz, Bildad, and Zophar. The image, nevertheless, elegantly conveys some of the main themes found in the lessons: the brevity of life and its miseries, the constant request for deliverance, and above all, the conviction of faith that permits one to declare he knows that his Redeemer liveth. In medieval lore Job's friends attempt to convince him to give up his faith, but he remains steadfast. Elegantly dressed, they are wealthy, as Job was before God permitted Satan to test his faith. Job is not moved, but patient, even though the youngest friend kneels in order to add direct eye contact to the persuasiveness of his argument. Although Poyet has depicted Job in a loincloth, he has not included the boils. According to Pope Gregory the Great (r. 590–604), Job sat on the dungheap so that he might consider the substance of the flesh and how quickly it returned to stench.

In the end, the discourse went in Job's favor, and his friends incurred the wrath of God who then instructed them, in a dramatic turnabout, to seek Job's intercession on their behalf, which he gave. Not surprisingly, some of the Church Fathers, such as Gregory the Great, regarded Job as a prophet of the general Resurrection of the Dead.

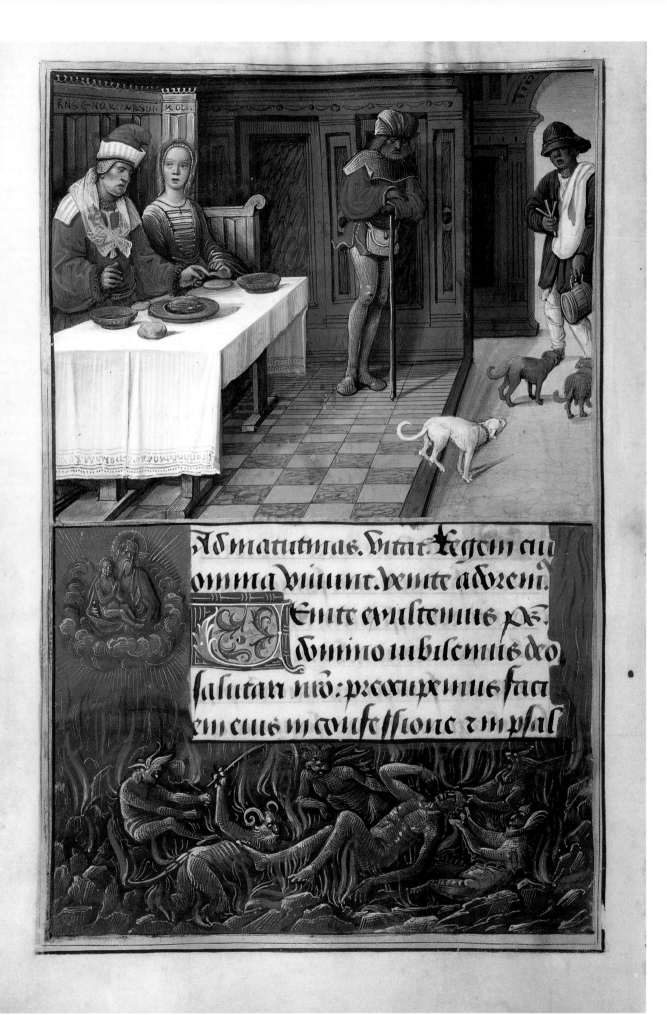

Matins: Feast of Dives
border: Dives in Hell (fol. 134v)

The second illustration for the Office of the Dead is smaller and is laid out like the Calendar and Suffrages, where half-page miniatures are in full color and marginal scenes in grisaille. The main subject, the Feast of Dives, derives from Luke's parable of the rich man (16:19–31). According to the story an unnamed rich man (Latin: *dives*) ate sumptuous meals every day, in full view of a poor man named Lazarus, who wanted only the crumbs that fell from his table. None, however, were given him, but the rich man's dogs came and licked his sores. The beggar died and was carried by angels to Abraham's bosom. The rich man, however, died and ended up in hell, where, in considerable torment, he lifted his eyes and saw Lazarus cradled by the patriarch. He then asked Abraham for Lazarus to dip the tip of his finger in water to cool his tongue, as he was tormented by the flames. Abraham replied that he had received good things in his lifetime while Lazarus had received evil things, but now Lazarus would be comforted while he would be tormented. It is, of course, significant that the poor man is worthy of being named while the rich man is not (this Lazarus, not to be confused with the Lazarus resurrected by Christ, has his feast day on June 21).

In the miniature the elegantly dressed rich man and his wife are about to enjoy a meal; Dives, who receives a glance from his wife, looks at Lazarus with disdain. A disinterested attendant stands nearby, while three dogs head toward Lazarus, who carries a small wooden keg and a clapper to warn passersby that he is a leper. Down below, in the flames of hell (appropriately painted in red grisaille), Dives sees Lazarus in the bosom of Abraham (in heavenly blue grisaille) and points to his mouth, a reference to his unfulfilled request.

SEVEN PRAYERS OF ST. GREGORY

(fols. 168v–169v)

As discussed above in connection with the accessory Prayers to the Virgin, in addition to the main texts of Books of Hours, a fairly large number of optional texts and prayers could be included, depending on the piety and pocketbook of the patron. Aside from individual prayers, these could include various Hours (of St. Catherine, of St. John the Baptist, and of the days of the week), special Masses (for saints and the days of the week), and a group of devotions organized around the number seven (Seven Joys of the Virgin, Seven Requests to Our Lord, Seven Last Words of Our Lord, Seven Verses of St. Bernard, and the present Seven Prayers of St. Gregory).

According to tradition the Seven Prayers were written by St. Gregory the Great, the fourth Latin Doctor of the Church (as the rubric for the prayers states in a contemporaneous Rouen *Horae* also in the Morgan Library's Heineman Collection: MS H.1, fol. 114v). The prayers consist of seven short ejaculations addressed to Christ, each followed by an Our Father and Hail Mary. The first begins:

O Domine Ih[es]u Xpisti adoro te in cruce pendente[m] et coronam spineam in capite portantem. Deprecor te ut crux tua liberet me ab angelo percutiente.

O Lord Jesus Christ, I adore you, hanging on the Cross and wearing the Crown of Thorns on your head. I beseech you so that your Cross might free me from the persecuting angel.

The other six prayers (all beginning *"O Domine Ih[es]u Xpisti adoro te . . ."*) relate to the bleeding Christ, the dying Christ, the Entombment, the Descent into Hell, the Resurrection, and Christ as the Good Shepherd. In the present manuscript the text is preceded by a rubric (fol. 167v) identifying it as a devotional prayer of the Vision of St. Gregory (*"Or[ati]o devota apparic[i]o[n]is s[an]c[t]i Gregorii"*).

—W.M.V.

Mass of St. Gregory (fol. 168)

The typical illustration for the Seven Prayers, the Mass of St. Gregory, was apparently invented in the fifteenth century. The initial seed for the story, a ninth-century biography of Gregory, was popularized in the *Golden Legend*. As Gregory was consecrating the Host during Mass, the woman who baked it laughed in disbelief that her kneaded dough would become the Body of Christ. Instead of giving her communion, he placed the wafer on the altar, praying to God for her unbelief. When the woman saw the host change into a piece of flesh in the form of a finger, she immediately rejoined the faithful; thereafter the flesh again became bread and she took communion. About 1400, however, owing to the growing emphasis on Christ's human suffering fostered by Franciscans—especially in the *Meditations on the Life of Christ*—the story circulated that the Man of Sorrows himself appeared on the altar. Around the same time a variant story developed to explain the thirteenth-century won-der-working mosaic icon of the *Imago pietatis* in Santa Croce in Gerusalemme in Rome. It was believed to have been commissioned by Gregory himself after, in a Mass, he asked God to change the wine into real blood; in that story Christ appeared on the altar and his blood flowed into the chalice.

In the miniature, St. Gregory, assisted by a deacon and subdeacon, elevates the consecrated Host during a High Mass. As is liturgically correct, the sub-deacon holds a torch, while the deacon lifts the back of Gregory's chasuble, which, like the altar frontal, is embroidered with the monogram of Jesus (IHS). Gregory, holding the wafer (itself decorated with the Crucifixion) between the first finger and thumb of both hands, recites the words *"Hoc est enim corpus meum"* (For this is my Body). At the same time, the live and bleeding Christ miraculously appears on the altar, supported by two angels above his sarcophagus. Against the blue background are the *arma christi* (arms of Christ), which were part of the Man of Sorrows iconography. A picto-graphic summary of Christ's Passion makes it possible for the devout to con-template the enormity of Christ's sufferings. The symbols include: the purse (Judas's betrayal for thirty pieces of silver), lantern (Christ was taken at night), sword (with which Peter cut off Malchus's ear), ewer and dish (with which Pilate washed his hands of guilt), cock (crowed when Peter denied he was a disciple of Christ), column with rope and two kinds of scourges (Flagellation), purple garment and Crown of Thorns (Mocking of Christ), Cross (Carrying of Cross), hammer and three nails in Cross with titulus (Crucifixion), three dice (soldiers gambled for Christ's garments), spear with sponge (Christ took vinegar), spear (Christ's side opened, with outpouring of blood and water), and pincers and ladder (for the Deposition).

fol. 168

SUFFRAGES

(fols. 170v–193)

Suffrages, prayers to saints seeking favor or support (also called Memorials), are frequently the last component in a Book of Hours. Petitionary or intercessory in nature, they normally consist of four elements: the first three, an antiphon, versicle, and response, make up a string of praises; the fourth part is a longer prayer *(oratio)* specifically dealing with some aspect of the saint, along with a request for God's aid through the saint's intercession. Many of these elements are quotations or extracts drawn from the Church's official liturgical texts found in the Breviary, which contained the rounds of offices recited by the clergy during the year, or in the Missal, which contained the Masses. The collect from the Mass and Office (Lauds) of St. Nicholas (6 December), for example, served as the *Oratio* for his Suffrage (fol. 182v); a translation of the entire Suffrage follows.

> **Antiphon.** *Nicholas, friend of God, when invested with the episcopal insignia, showed himself a friend to all.*
> **Versicle.** *Pray for us, blessed Nicholas.*
> **Response.** *That we may be made worthy of the promises of Christ.*
> **Oratio.** *O God, you adorned the pious blessed bishop Nicholas with countless miracles; grant, we beseech you, that through his merits and prayers, we may be delivered from the flames of hell. Through Jesus Christ our Lord.*

The justification and efficacy of such petitions to the saints had already been established by the fourth century and were unequivocally reaffirmed in the thirteenth century by Thomas Aquinas in his *Summa theologica*. In raising the question if one should pray to God alone, he referred to Job (5:l), where Eliphaz exhorted him to call upon some of the saints; to show that the saints in heaven could

indeed pray for us Aquinas also quoted Jerome: "If the apostles and martyrs while yet in body can pray for others, how much more now that they have the crown of victory and triumph." In asking if prayer to greater saints was more acceptable to God than to lesser saints, Aquinas said it was sometimes more profitable to pray to a lesser saint, since some saints were granted special patronage in certain areas, such as St. Anthony against the fires of hell. Moreover, he added, the effect of prayer depended on one's devotion, and that could be greater for a lesser saint.

Aquinas also alluded to another common custom of the Church to support his conclusions, the recitation of the Litany of saints (a practice dating back to the fourth century). It is the celestial hierarchy of saints in the Litany, moreover, that provides the basic ordering of the Suffrages in Books of Hours. Indeed, in the present manuscript, all of the Suffrages are illustrated, forming a kind of pictorial Litany (albeit a very selective one). After the Three Persons of the Trinity comes the Archangel Michael, followed by John the Baptist (our future intercessor at the Last Judgment). Next are the apostles, male martyrs, confessors (male nonmartyr saints), female martyrs, and widows. The series concludes with All Saints. (It may be of interest to observe that the first five female saints precisely follow the order in which they appear in the manuscript's Litany.) The idea of placing large miniatures of the saints above the Suffrages, with other scenes from the life of the saint in different colored grisailles in the lower borders, brings full circle the page layout of the Calendar and Gospel Lessons at the beginning of the manuscript. The number of Suffrages in Books of Hours can vary greatly, and each one is not always illustrated; the series of twenty-four in the present manuscript is particularly rich, and bespeaks a fairly wealthy patron.

The placement of Jerome at the beginning of the Suffrages is highly unusual. His position here may have been intended to link Jerome with Pope Gregory, the Church Father who was believed to have written the previous text (Seven Prayers of St. Gregory). In addition, Jerome's Suffrage, as is clear from the translation below, emphasizes his role as a teacher rather than as a penitent.

Antiphon. *I shall liken him to a wise man who built his house on rock.*

Versicle. *The Lord led the just man in right paths.*

Response. *And showed him the kingdom of God.*

Oratio. *O God, who didst vouchsafe to provide for thy Church blessed Jerome, thy confessor, a great doctor for the expounding of the Sacred Scriptures, grant, we beseech thee, that through his merits we may be enabled, by thine assistance, to practice what by word and deed he hath taught us. Through Our Lord Jesus Christ thy Son, who liveth and reigneth, God, with thee, in the unity of the Holy Spirit, world without end. Amen.*

Since the accompanying picture of Jerome in Penance is, like the Mass of Gregory, a full-page miniature (all of the other Suffrages are half-page miniatures with historiated borders), it could be seen as a kind of frontispiece for the Suffrage section. In any case, Jerome and Gregory were both Latin Doctors of the Church, and both miniatures focus on the crucified body of Christ. Codicological evidence and the rubric for the Suffrage ("De sancto Ieronimo") would indicate that the present placement was intended, suggesting that Jerome had some special significance for the patron. Pictures of Jerome in Penance became increasingly popular at this time: a similar image by the Master of Claude de France, for example, was inserted in the 1510s to Poyet's Hours of Mary of England, probably by King Louis XII when he had the book remodeled for his last wife (as discussed on pp. 26–27).

—K.M.H. & W.M.V.

St. Jerome: Jerome in Penance (fol. 170)

Jerome, considered the most learned of the Latin Church fathers, was born around 342 in the small town of Stridon in Dalmatia. Well-educated, he was sent to Rome as a youth to study the Greek and Latin classics with the pagan grammarian, Donatus. Baptized and later ordained as a priest, Jerome made a pilgrimage to the Holy Land. In Antioch he decided to retire as a hermit in the Syrian Desert, where he suffered temptations of the flesh. In a letter to his friend Eustachium, he recounted how in the heat of the sun, with no other companions besides scorpions and wild beasts, he imagined Roman maidens dancing before him. To avoid these temptations, as shown here, he threw himself amid thorn bushes before a crucifix, beat his breast (the rock was a later medieval invention), and fled into the wilderness for four years.

In 382, he returned to Rome, where he produced the standard text of the Latin Bible (the Vulgate) before moving to Bethlehem, founding a monastic settlement of contemplative hermits with St. Paula (the Hieronymite Order).

One evening, according to one legend, as Jerome sat within the gates of his monastery, a lion entered, limping in pain. The saint removed a thorn in its paw, tending the lion's wound until it healed. The beast became one of the saint's attributes.

Although Jerome was never a cardinal (the office did not yet exist), he is depicted as one. Here the cardinal's cloak and hat lie on the ground so we can see his hair shirt. Images of the penitent Jerome in the wilderness originated in Pisa during the late thirteenth/early fourteenth centuries. The motif of the saint beating his breast with a stone—which first occurs in a fourteenth-century panel in Pisa (Galleria San Matteo)—was adopted in the North at the end of the fifteenth century. Scenes of Jerome in the wilderness also afforded the artist an opportunity to explore nature, landscape, and wildlife—features exploited by Poyet. (Feast day: September 30)

Trinity: Trinity
border: Angels (fol. 171)

The Christian conception of a triune God, each part equal and indistinguishable, is the subject of this miniature. The Three Persons of God, seated on a golden rainbow within an aureole surrounded by clouds, are physically and hierarchically identical: they each appear as a young Christ holding an orb. It is tempting to identify the central blessing figure as God the Father, flanked by Christ at his right hand (as in the Apostles' and Nicene Creeds) and the Holy Spirit at his left. The Athanasian Creed (sometimes called the *"Quicunque vult"* from its opening words in Latin), which specifically emphasizes the equality of the Three Persons of the Trinity, is included as the last text in the Hours of Henry VIII (fols. 196–199v). The number of the nine celestial angels kneeling in adoration and prayer below may recall the nine orders of angels.

Trinity Sunday, the feast day dedicated to the Trinity, was not originally celebrated in the early Christian Church. Although it was observed regionally in the tenth century, it was not universally accepted until 1334, when Pope John XXII (r. 1316–34) ordered it to be generally observed. (Feast day: the first Sunday after Pentecost, or the eighth Sunday after Easter)

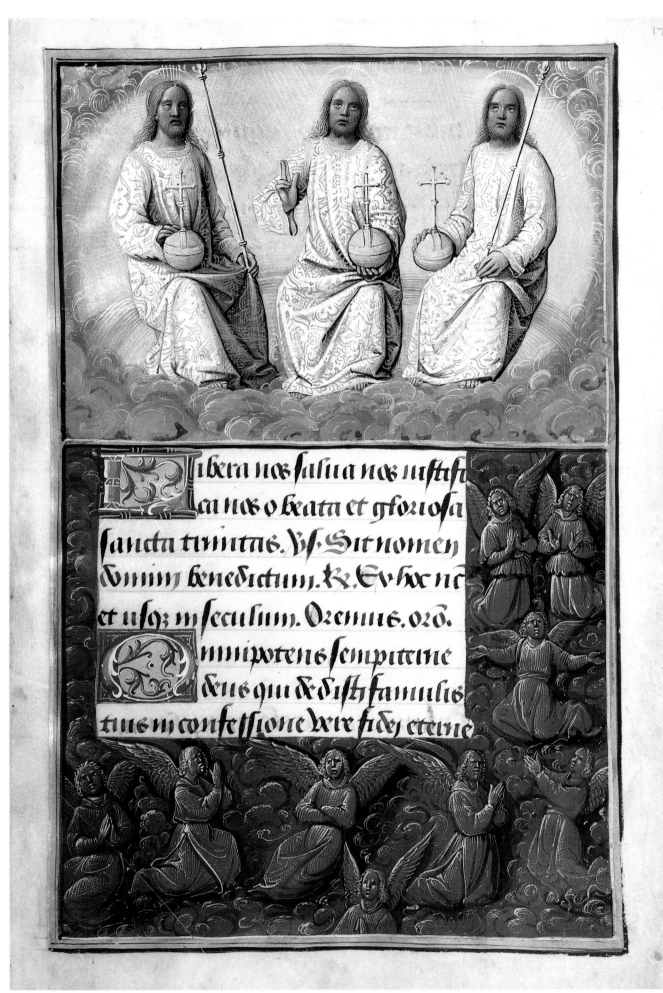

St. Michael the Archangel: Michael Battling a Devil
border: Fall of the Rebel Angels (fol. 172)

Archangel Michael is God's commander-in-chief in the war against the Devil. In his dramatic confrontation with Satan at the beginning of time, Michael defeated his army and hurled the fallen angel and his minions into hell. At the end of the world it is said that Michael will return to earth for his final battle with the Antichrist. The archangel's second duty will be to weigh the souls of the departed and determine if they can enter heaven.

Michael's cult began in the East where he was invoked for care of the sick (Constantine built a church near Constantinople for this purpose). A fifth-century apparition on Monte Gargano (in southeast Italy) was important in spreading the cult to the West. In the later Middle Ages, the Valois dynasty of French kings adopted him as their patron saint.

Throughout the Middle Ages the archangel's iconography varied. We know him best in armor or at least minimally carrying a shield (as here) while slaying the Devil in the form of a dragon or demon. With a cross-surmounted spear Michael stabs the defeated Satan, who is garbed in antique-style armor (a convention Poyet acquired while visiting Italy). In the margin below, Satan's corps of rebellious angels, changed into demons, fall into the flames of hell.

Michael is sometimes confused with St. George, who also slew a dragon, but there is an easy way to distinguish the two. George, a canonized human, is never depicted with wings, while Michael, an archangel, always has them. (Feast day: September 29, Michaelmas)

ichael archangele ben̄ı ad
iutorium p̄puło deı et belıɔ
nos deffendere a p̄testate ınımıcı et
tecum ducere ın socıetatem dm̄ınɔ.
V̧. Jn conspectu angelorum pſal
lam tıbı, deus meus. Ŗ. Adorabo ad
templum sanctum tuum et confite

St. John the Baptist: Baptism of Christ
border: John the Baptist Preaching (fol. 173)

The Archangel Gabriel told John's elderly parents, Zacharias, a Jewish priest, and Elizabeth, the Virgin Mary's cousin, that they would have a son, named John. After Gabriel informed Mary that she, too, would have a son, the two women visited each other (the Visitation); on that occasion John leaped in his mother's womb at the presence of the yet unborn Jesus. Although the *Golden Legend* says they were childhood playmates, John and Jesus did not meet again until manhood.

Around A.D. 27, John moved to the desert of Judea near the river Jordan, where he preached penance, the coming kingdom of God, and baptism for the remission of sins; he lived on locusts and wild honey, and wore a camel's hair. He baptized Jesus in the river, recognizing him as the Redeemer when the Holy Spirit appeared above him in the form of a dove. In the miniature, an angel waits on the opposite bank with Christ's robe.

John's outspoken preaching led to his martyrdom. He publicly censured Governor Herod Antipas for his incestuous marriage with his brother's wife and was subsequently imprisoned in the fortress of Machaerus. The dancer Salome, who had attracted Herod's notice through her dancing at his birthday feast, demanded and received the Baptist's head on a platter.

The saint is normally depicted wearing a leather girdle and a garment made from camel's hair, but Poyet has clothed him in a camel skin instead, with the camel's head and even a paw bumping about the saint's knees. John's long hair and scruffy beard identify him as a hermit. Below, in the margin, John preaches to the multitude in a forest, his pulpit formed by a branch horizontally attached to two tree trunks. (Feast day: June 24)

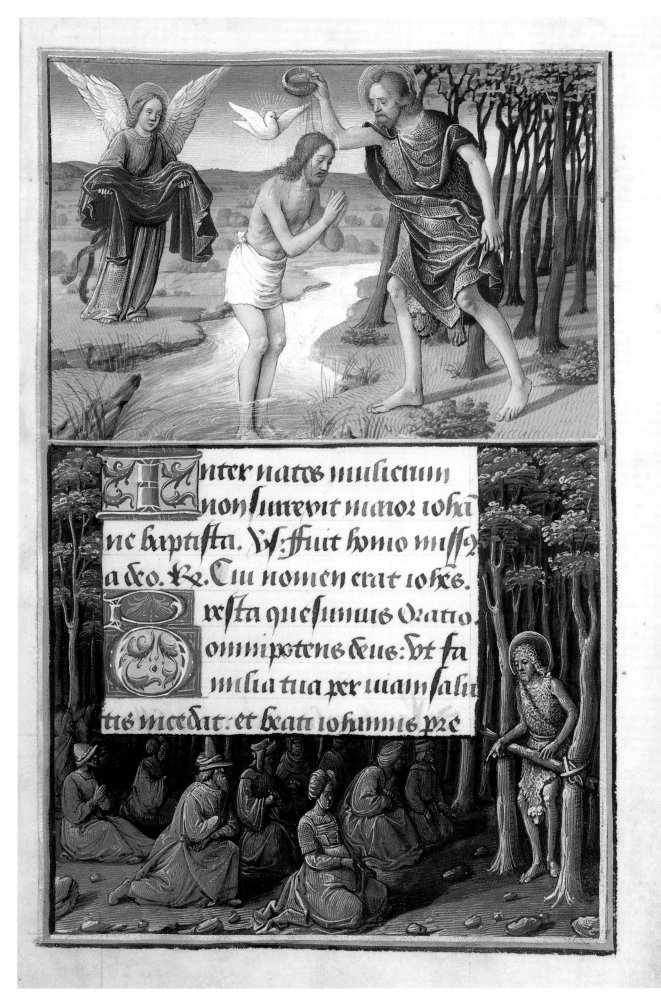

nter natos mulienum
non surrexit maior iohā
ne baptista. V̄ʃ. fuit homo miʃʃꝫ
a deo. Rc. Cui nomen erat ioħꝫ.
resta quesumus Oratio
omnipotens deus: vt fa
milia tua per uiam salu
tis incedat: et beati iohannis pre

St. John the Evangelist: John the Evangelist Descending into his Grave
  into his Grave
border: John and the Beast of the Apocalypse (fol. 174)

In the first year of his teaching, Christ called John the Evangelist (son of Zebedee) and his younger brother, St. James the Elder, while they were mending their fishing nets on the Sea of Galilee. Originally disciples of John the Baptist, they became followers of Jesus. John witnessed the Transfiguration and the Agony in the Garden with Peter and James, and was the "beloved disciple" who fell asleep on the bosom of Christ at the Last Supper. The only disciple not to forsake the Savior during the Passion, he was made the guardian of Jesus' mother, Mary, and was thought to have cared for her until her death.

John was a prominent figure in the early Church. He preached in Samaria and Jerusalem with St. Peter and traveled on to Rome from where he was presumably exiled to Patmos under the persecution of Emperor Domitian. Tradition (but not modern scholarship) says that on this island he wrote the Apocalypse, or Book of Revelation, based on visions he experienced there.

After Domitian's death (A.D. 96), John went to Ephesus. There Aristodemus, high priest of Diana, challenged him to drink a cup of poisoned wine as a test of his God's strength. John blessed the cup, and the poison departed in the form of a serpent.

The youngest of the apostles, the Evangelist survived all of the apostles and lived to the ripe old age of about 101. As his end neared, according to the *Golden Legend,* Jesus appeared and called him. John had a grave dug near the altar of his church and then, as in the miniature, walked into it. He said a prayer, a bright light surrounded him, and the saint vanished, leaving the grave filled with manna. In the lower margin, John blesses the poisoned cup, from which serpents slither. Across a narrow body of water is the seven-headed beast of the Apocalypse. (Feast day: December 27)

Iohannes apostolus et euan
gelista uirgo est electus.
atqz inter ceteros magis dilectus.
V. Valde honorandus est beatus
iohannes. R. Qui supra pectus do
mini in cena recubuit. Oratio
ecclesiam tuam quesumus
domine benignus illust

Sts. Peter and Paul: Fall of Simon Magus
border: Decapitation of Paul and Crucifixion of Peter (fol. 175)

Simon Peter, another fisherman turned apostle, was known as the "rock of the Church." The Gospels record Christ's words to him, "Thou art Peter, and upon this rock I will build my church, and the gates of Hades shall not prevail against it; I will give unto thee the keys of the kingdom of Heaven." These words are also the source for Peter's attribute, a large key. One of the three apostles who witnessed Christ's Transfiguration, he traveled to Antioch after the Resurrection and preached the Gospel until A.D. 42. Peter was the first bishop of Rome and suffered martyrdom there. Nero ordered his crucifixion on 29 June 64, in his circus below the Vatican Hill. Considering himself unworthy to die as Jesus had, the saint insisted upon being crucified head downward.

Paul, formerly a Greek-Jewish tentmaker named Saul, was a strict Pharisee and persecuted the young Christian Church fanatically until an apparition of the resurrected Christ on the road to Damascus converted him. After he returned to Rome, he was beheaded by Nero on the road to Ostia, on the same day as Peter's martyrdom.

According to the Apocryphal Acts of Peter, there was a sorcerer in Jerusalem named Simon Magus who proclaimed himself the source of truth and promised immortality to his believers. He confronted Peter to prove that he was God, but the apostle refuted and exposed him. So the sorcerer went to Rome and gained Nero's support. Simon called the people together and declared that he was offended by Peter and Paul's presence in the city; he threatened to abandon Rome and ascend into heaven. Climbing a tower, he rose in flight, while Nero accused the two apostles of being imposters. Peter, pointing out the flying sorcerer to Paul, cried out, "Angels of Satan, who hold this man up in the air, in the name of my Master Jesus Christ, I command you to hold him up no longer!" As shown in the miniature, they obeyed and Simon promptly plunged to his death. The disgruntled emperor then cast the two saints into prison, condemning them to death.

Although their executions did not occur at the same location, they are often depicted together, as in the margin, since they happened (and are thus celebrated) on the same day. Even without attributes, it is possible to distinguish between Peter and Paul by their appearance. Peter traditionally has a square, bald head with a short rectangular beard, and Paul a bulbous forehead, narrow chin, and a long beard. (Feast day: June 29)

etrus apostolus et paulus
doctor gentium ipsi nos d=
ocuerunt legem tuam domine. Vs
In omnem terram exiuit sonus eo=
rum. Ro Et in fines orbis terre ver=
ba eorum. Oremus. Oratio.
eus cuius dextera beatum
petrum apostolum ambu=

St. James: James with Hermogenes
border: Decapitation of James (fol. 176)

James the Greater, or Elder (he was the older of two apostles named James), was the brother of John the Evangelist. After Christ's Ascension, James preached in Judea and Samaria, and then went to Spain. After he returned to Judea, the Pharisees requested that the magician Hermogenes should send his disciple, Philetus, to confront and refute James. The saint performed some miracles, however, resulting in the conversion of Philetus and the rage of Hermogenes, who then ordered two demons to capture James and Philetus. Warned of the plot, the saint prayed that the demons bind and deliver Hermogenes instead, which they did. Here Poyet has rendered the demons holding Hermogenes as exotically dressed soldiers while the converted Philetus looks on. The terrified magician repented and promised to destroy his magic books. Afraid of the demons, Hermogenes asked for something that belonged to the saint to prevent their attack, so James gave him his staff; when the converted magician returned with his tomes, the apostle threw them into the sea. The disappointed Pharisees dragged the saint before Herod Agrippa, who condemned him to be beheaded (A.D. 43). This story is apparently modeled on that of Peter and Simon Magus in the preceding narrative. In the margin below, a crowd of kneeling men and women witness James's decapitation.

After James's death, angels transported his body to Spain where it lay on a stone that closed over it. His relics were discovered in the year 800 and taken to Compostella, which became a major pilgrimage site in the Middle Ages. Pilgrims would return with badges as souvenirs, especially scallop shells (cockleshells); these were valued and often handed down as legacies. By the late Middle Ages, the saint himself was depicted as a pilgrim—his costume including a satchel decorated with a shell, a large hat, a traveler's cape, and staff—in the miniature two scallop shells decorate James's hat. (Feast day: July 25)

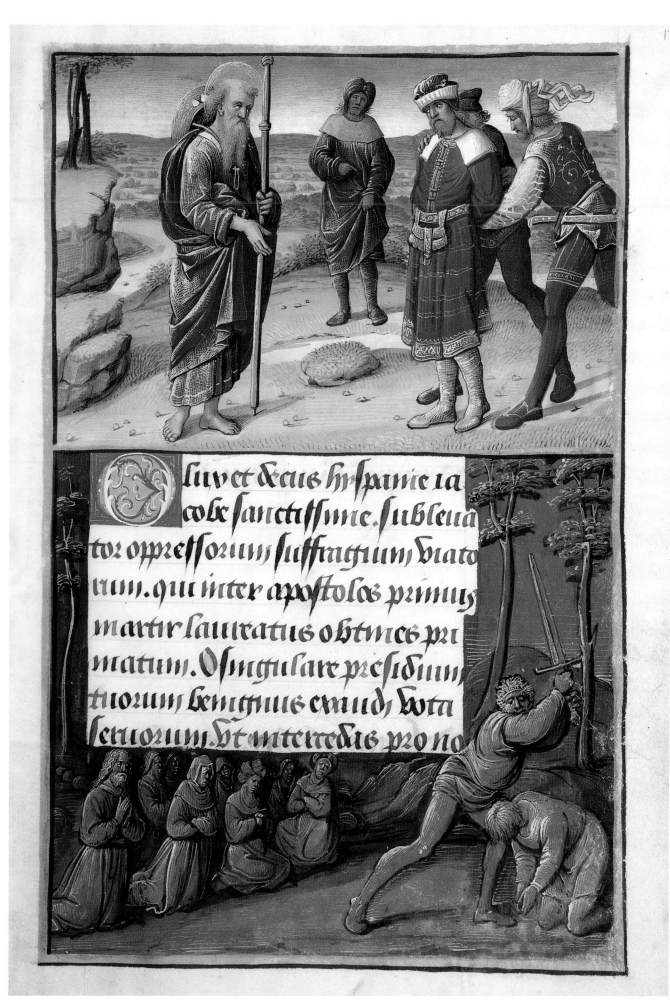

lus et deus hyspanie ia
cobe sanctissime. subleua
tor oppressorum suffragium viato
rum. qui inter apostolos primus
martir laureatus obtines pri
matum. O singulare presidium
tuorum benigniue exaudi vota
seruorum. sit intercessio pro no

St. Philip: Philip Vanquishing Idols and a Demon
border: Philip Baptizing (fol. 177)

Philip, a native of Bethsaida in Galilee and a married father of three, gave up everything to follow Jesus. In the apostle's most famous miracle, he cast the Devil, in the form of a hideous dragon, out of a statue of Mars. A group of Scythian pagans had attempted to force the saint to sacrifice to a statue of the god Mars, but a huge dragon suddenly emerged from the statue, slaying the son of the priest and the two tribunes who had arrested the saint. The noxious breath of the beast sickened onlookers. Philip told the crowd that if they broke the statue and adored the Lord's Cross, the sick would be cured and the dead would be brought back to life. The crowd agreed, and the saint spoke to the dragon, sending it to a desert far away. Philip then healed the injured and revived the dead, converting the entire city.

In the miniature, a horned demon (instead of the traditional dragon) flees from Philip and four statues fall from the altar of Mars (the golden ones are men, the white ones women). Beneath the demon are the fallen bodies of the sick and wounded, soon to be restored to health. In the image below, the saint baptizes the first of a long line of new converts made as a result of the miracle. (Feast day: May 1)

anto tempore vobiscu
sum et non cognou
istis me philippe. qui videt me
videt et patrem meum. Vers. Ora
pro nobis beate philippe. Resp.
Ut digni efficiamur promis
sionibus christi. Oremus.
Oratio.

St. Christopher: Conversion of Christopher
border: Christopher Carrying Christ (fol. 178)

Christopher's name, which means "Christ-bearer," seems to be the basis of his legend. Christopher, a Canaanite named Reprobus before his baptism, was a fearsome giant of a man. Deciding to serve only the most powerful lord on earth, he became a follower of Satan. However, the Devil fled upon seeing a crucifix planted in the roadway. Seeing Satan's fear, the giant resolved to follow Christ and his Cross instead. The miniature shows the moment when the saint embraced Christianity, acknowledging the Cross's power with a reverential glance and hand gesture. The Devil on horseback gallops away in terror.

A hermit subsequently instructed the newly baptized Christopher in the Christian faith and gave him the task of helping travelers across a river. One stormy night a child asked the saint's assistance in traversing the current. The child was so heavy on Christopher's back that he nearly did not manage to cross. On the opposite bank the child announced that he was Jesus and that Christopher had just carried the weight of the entire world on his shoulders. As proof of this, the child commanded the saint to plant his staff in the ground so that on the next day it would blossom with flowers and dates.

In the margin, with the young Christ Child perched on his back, the saint struggles to cross the raging river. He leans heavily on his staff, panting with exertion. On the opposite bank is his mentor, the old hermit, who holds a lantern to light the way. (Feast day: formerly July 14)

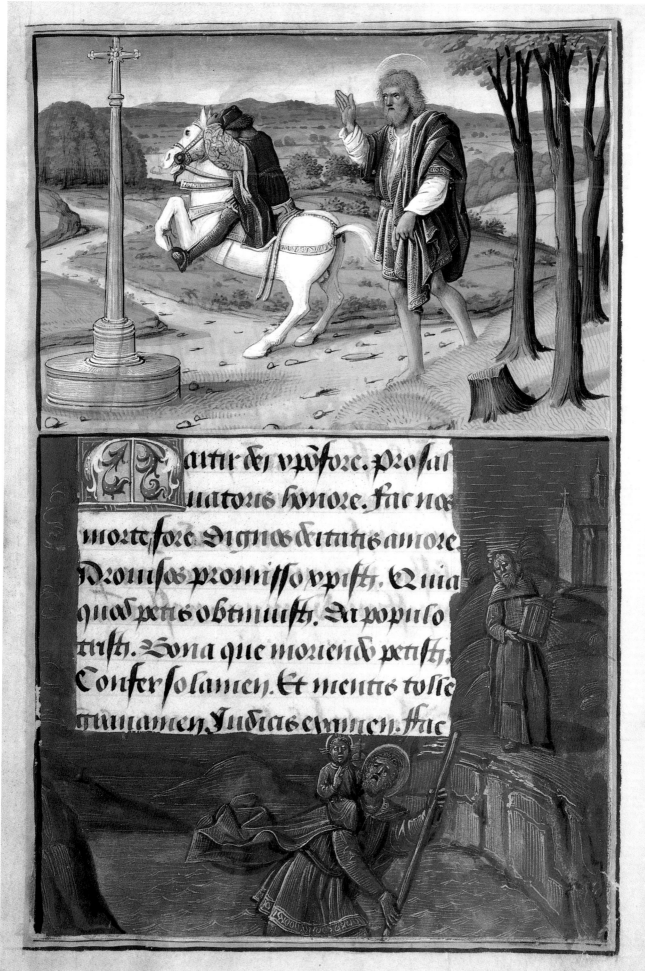

artir dei vputore. pro sal
uatoris honore. fac nos
morte fore dignos & intis amore.
Da nobis promissa ypisti. Quia
quas petis obtinuisti. Ai populo
tristi. Bona que moriendo petisti.
Confer solamen. Et mentis tolle
grauamen. Judicis exameri. fac

St. Sebastian: Sebastian Shot with Arrows, Abandoned by Archers border: Sebastian's Body Cast into the Sewer (fol. 179)

According to legend, Sebastian was born in Gaul and raised in Milan. Although a Christian, he joined the Roman army in 283, rising to captain in the Praetorian Guard under Emperor Diocletian. He clandestinely assisted and consoled imprisoned Christians in addition to converting and baptizing other soldiers and civilians. His own religious convictions remained a secret until the tortures inflicted on his Christian friends Marcus and Marcellinus so infuriated him that he publicly proclaimed his faith. He was then condemned to die as a target for archery practice. After the attack, a pious widow, Irene, claimed the body but discovered that Sebastian was still alive. She nursed him back to health, and he returned to the palace to confront the emperor. Diocletian promptly ordered Sebastian beaten to death and the body dumped into the Cloaca Maxima, the main sewer of Rome, preventing Christians from preserving and venerating it as the relic of a martyr. On the following night, however, the saint appeared to a Roman matron, St. Lucina, revealing the location of his body, which was subsequently retrieved and interred in the catacomb on the Old Appian Way. In the lower margin two men dump Sebastian's shrouded body into the sewer. To the right a figure leaning on his staff, probably the emperor, oversees the operation, while at the left three Christians, including the matron Lucina, wait to reclaim the body.

During the late Middle Ages, Sebastian was usually depicted as a handsome, beardless youth, bound to a stake and pierced with arrows, his eyes looking heavenward. From the fifteenth century on he was nude (or nearly so). Poyet's Sebastian, muscular, his eyes turned upward, and clothed in a suggestively tied loincloth, is based on an Italian model. (Feast day: January 20)

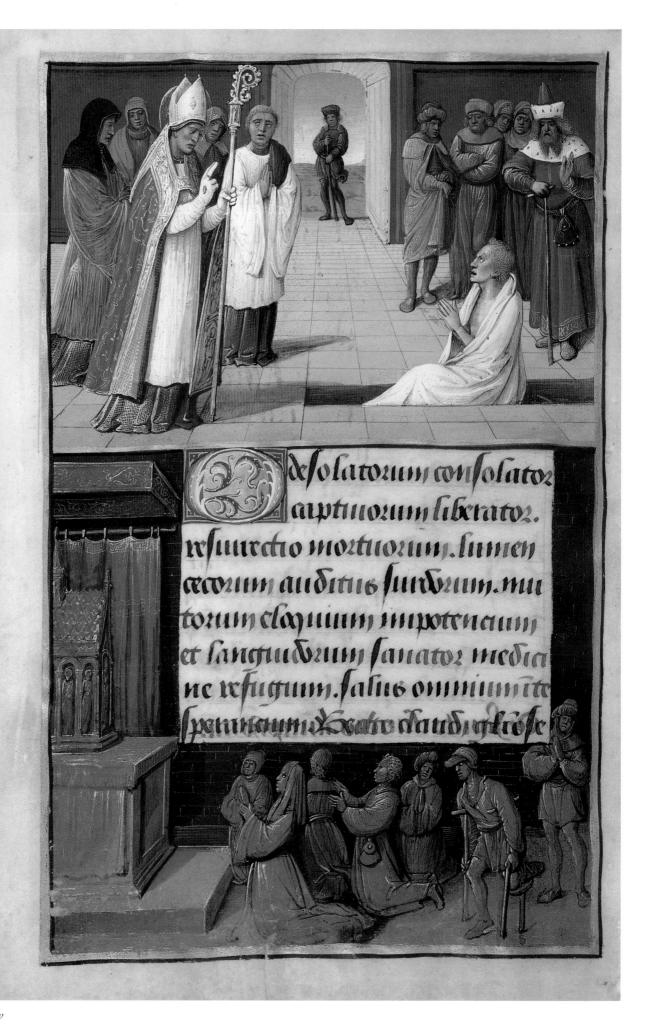

desolatorium consolator
captinorum liberator.
resurrectio mortuorum. lumen
cecorum auditus surdorum. mu
torum eloquium impotencium
et sanguidrum sanator media
ne refugium. salus omnium te
sperancium. beato claudius esse

*St. Claude of Besançon: Claude Resuscitating a Dead Man
border: Pilgrims Kneeling before Claude's Shrine* (fol. 180v)

Born at Salins in 607, Claude of Besançon was said to be from a Roman
senatorial family. At the age of twenty he gave up a military career to
become canon of Besançon; later he became a monk at the monastery of
St. Oyend in the Jura Mountains, where he was subsequently elected abbot.
As abbot, Claude applied the rule of St. Benedict and restored the
monastery's buildings. In 685, he was chosen bishop of Besançon but retired
eight years later to Condate, where he died and was buried (6 June 699).
His burial place (later called Saint-Claude) was a popular pilgrimage site and
miraculous cures took place there, including the resuscitation of three
drowned children and a dead boy.

Claude, as in the miniature, is usually depicted as a bishop with miter and
crosier. Here, as a result of his blessing, a dead man sits up in his grave, newly
restored to life. (Legends often mention a dead child.) Below, a group of pilgrims worship before the jewel-encrusted *chasse* containing the saint's relics.
A woman in contemporary court dress kneels in front. Claude was often
prayed to by French nobility for the birth of sons. At the rear hobbles a crip-
ple, hoping for his eventual cure. (Feast day: June 6)

fol. 181v

St. Adrian: Martyrdom of Adrian
border: Christians in Prison (fol. 181v)

Adrian (or Hadrian) was a young Praetorian Guard in Nicomedia under Emperor Maximian (r. 286–305). The soldier was converted by witnessing the steadfast confidence of a group of Christians under torture. Impressed by their constancy, he asked to be counted among their ranks. Needless to say, Adrian was promptly arrested and imprisoned. His new wife Natalia (a secret Christian) was overjoyed, ran to the prison, and encouraged him to remain firm in his new faith, kissing his chains. When he learned the date of his impending martyrdom, the saint convinced the guards to allow him to tell his wife so that she could witness the event.

On the day of his death (c. 300), Adrian was first beaten so severely that his "bowels fell out." After he was returned to prison, the emperor ordered that the legs of all the imprisoned martyrs be broken on an anvil and cut off. Natalia, who was present, additionally requested that the guards cut off her husband's hands, so that he would be equal to other saints who had suffered more. After Adrian's death, Natalia managed to get away with a hand (holding it to her bosom), taking it with her to Argyropolis where she died peacefully.

The miniature shows Adrian's two-part martyrdom. He is seated on the anvil, his intestines having already fallen out, as two executioners begin to hack off his legs. Adrian looks heavenward, while in the background Natalia prays contentedly; the emperor, at the left, directs the martyrdom. In the margin, a jailer guards the imprisoned Christians who prompted Adrian's conversion. (Feast day: September 8, the translation of his relics to Rome)

St. Nicholas: Nicholas Giving Gold to the Three Maidens
border: Nicholas Resuscitating the Three Boys (fol. 182v)

Nicholas (of Myra or Bari), one of the most universally venerated saints, is said to have been born about 270 and died in 342. A precociously religious child of wealthy parents, Nicholas supposedly stood up and praised God the moment he was born. When he inherited his father's fortune, he gave it away to the poor. His most celebrated act of generosity occurred upon hearing an impoverished neighbor lament that he could not supply dowries for his three daughters, leaving them no alternative but a life of prostitution. On three successive nights Nicholas threw a bag of gold (or a gold ball) through their window. In the miniature the saint appears at a double window holding a bag of gold near a bed while the girls' despondent father slumps in a chair. (The three gold balls became the insignia for the pawnbroker.)

The saint's second famous miracle involves an unscrupulous innkeeper who, during a food shortage, dismembered and pickled three young boys to feed his guests. Sensing foul play, Nicholas made the sign of the Cross over the tub, and the three stood up restored to life. In the grisaille border, the three boys, now restored, kneel in gratitude before the blessing saint. This legend may have developed from the three purses or gold balls normally shown with the saint, which were mistaken for the tow heads of children.

As Nicholas's feast falls during the Christmas season, he was confused with a folklore character who rewarded good children with gifts brought secretly during the night. The two eventually merged to become Father Christmas or Santa Claus. (Feast day: December 6)

nthoni pastor incite qui
lauciatus refras mor bus sa
nas et desuiis igms caloren evti
guis pie piter ad dommum ora pro
nobis miseris. V. Ora pro nobis
beate piter anthoni. R. Ut digni
eus qui coneedis Oratio.
obtentu beati anthonii

St. Anthony Abbot: Temptation of Anthony
border: Anthony in the Wilderness (fol. 183v)

Anthony Abbot, or Anthony the Great (c. 251–356), is best known for his long life of asceticism in the Egyptian deserts. Born in an Egyptian village near Memphis, he decided at age twenty, when his parents died, to become a hermit. For two decades the saint lived in complete solitude in an abandoned tomb. Here the Devil tempted him in the form of an attractive woman, and scared him in the forms of a black man and then wild animals.

In 1095, in La Motte (in southern France), an order of Hospitalers was created in the saint's honor. Wearing black robes with a blue tau cross, they traveled ringing bells for alms. By special ordinance, the Hospitalers' pigs were allowed to forage freely, leading to pictures of the saint accompanied by a pig.

In the miniature, Anthony appears as a bearded old man in a black robe and tau cross (the Egyptian cross and a symbol of his abbatial authority). The crutch at the saint's feet refers both to Christ's Cross and to the Hospitalers' care of the infirm. Anthony reaches toward the fire (the disease ergotism was known as St. Anthony's fire) to escape the demonic young woman (note her horns). In the margin below, the saint appears with his staff in the wilderness; the open book symbolizes the book of nature, which compensated the saint for lack of any other reading material. The belled pig at his side refers to the order of Hospitalers, but it was also his only companion in the wilderness. (Feast day: January 17)

alue fancte pater prīe
fux forma mmorum
vīrtutē fpeailum rectis vīa re
gula morum carnis ab ebilio duc
nos ad regna polorum. Vſ. Ora
pro nobis beate fmnaſce. Ře. Vt
eus qui eccleſiam Oro.
tuam beati franaſa me

St. Francis: Stigmatization of Francis
border: Francis in the Fiery Chariot (fol. 184v)

A great deal is known about the life of Francis of Assisi (1181–1226), the founder of the Order of Friars Minor (Franciscans). As a youth he led the life of a carefree cavalier, but a year spent as a prisoner of war in Perugia (1201) and a subsequent serious illness changed Francis's values, leading him to become a monk devoted to the care of the poor and lepers. In 1210, the saint, with a dozen followers, traveled to Rome, petitioning Pope Innocent III to establish his new order, the brotherhood of poverty. The order was created and rapidly grew.

On 14 September 1224, while on retreat at Mount Alvernia, Francis prayed that he might feel with his own body the agony of Christ on the Cross and was rewarded with the stigmata, which he hid from others until his death. The event, appropriately, occurred on the feast day of the Exaltation of the True Cross. Francis died two years later; he was canonized by Pope Gregory IX (r. 1227–41) in 1228.

The miniature shows the moment of stigmatization. Francis kneels in prayer on a mountaintop before the apparition of a seraph who folds his wings to form the shape of a cross. Five rays shoot out from the angel marking the saint in the same places as Christ's wounds. Francis wears the gray habit of his order with a cord for a belt. The knotted belt is a reminder of the cords that bound Christ; the three knots symbolize the three Franciscan virtues of poverty, chastity, and obedience. On the left is one of the three monks who went with Francis to the mountaintop, but who slept through the event.

The grisaille scene below depicts an obscure miracle—derived from Elijah's chariot of fire—that was popularized during the fourteenth century. Francis, concerned that his monks had been lax, appeared to them in a floating fiery chariot, reminding them to follow his rules of poverty and humility. The apparition awakens the monks, some of whom are still befuddled by sleep; two in the right rear, however, kneel in prayer. (Feast day: October 4)

161

St. Anthony of Padua: Anthony and the Miracle of the
  Kneeling Horse
border: Anthony Preaching (fol. 185v)

Although born in Lisbon in 1195, he is known as Anthony of Padua because
the basilica in that city (where he briefly resided) possesses his miracle-
working relics. Already, as a pious youth, he used prayer to overcome the
severe temptations against purity that he suffered during his teens. Initially
joining the Augustinian order, he later became a Franciscan friar.

Anthony had a magnificent memory and a vast knowledge of the Bible
and was acclaimed for his skill in preaching, which began when a misun-
derstanding at an ordination left the service without a speaker. His superi-
ors ordered him to come forward and say whatever the Holy Spirit put into
his mouth, which he did with great style, passion, and erudition. Anthony
preached throughout northern Italy and southern France with great success.

He died in 1231 at Arcella, near Padua, and was quickly canonized by
Pope Gregory IX the following year. Until the end of the fourteenth century his cult was a local Paduan phenomenon. However, in the fifteenth
century, Bernardino of Siena, a noted theologian and leader of the
Franciscan order, brought Anthony wider renown, making him the most
popular Franciscan saint after Francis of Assisi.

One of Anthony's most popular miracles involved a challenge to prove
the real presence of Christ in the Eucharist. The unbelieving man, a Jew
named Guillard, would be convinced if a horse could pass up a measure of
oats for the consecrated Host. Although the story is normally told about a
mule, Poyet has replaced it with a horse, who ignores the proffered feed and
kneels before the host that Anthony holds over a chalice. Guillard, at right,
looks on in astonishment. (Feast day: June 13)

eleste beneficium intro=
uit in anniam per quam
nobis nata est maria virgo. Vss.
Ora pro nobis beata anna. R̃. Vt
digni efficiamur promissioibz v.
eus qui beate anne Oro.
tantam gratiam et beati
tudinem conferre dignatus es: ut

St. Anne: Anne Instructing the Virgin
border: Presentation of the Virgin in the Temple (fol. 186v)

According to the apocryphal Gospel of James, the Virgin Mary's parents, Anne and Joachim, were an elderly and childless couple. An angel answered their prayers for a child, telling them that their offspring would become famous. Anne vowed to dedicate the infant Mary to the Lord, and at the age of three, the girl was presented in the Temple where she was raised in the service of God. Once Mary was old enough to marry, the priests sent her home so that she might find a husband.

In the later Middle Ages (with its increased literacy levels) Anne is increasingly depicted, as here, instructing the Virgin how to read. The scene takes place in a domestic interior that also includes other students, but Mary is distinguished by her primacy and her halo.

Below is Mary's presentation at the Temple. The three-year-old child, followed by Anne and Joachim but not assisted by them, has begun to climb the fifteen steps leading up to the temple. Zacharias, priest and father of John the Baptist, waits to receive her in the doorway.

According to the *Golden Legend,* Anne married twice after Joachim's death: first to Cleophas and then Salome, bearing a daughter named Mary to each of them. Each of her daughters named Mary, respectively bore one, four, and two sons, making Anne the grandmother of Jesus; Sts. Simon, Jude, Joseph the Just, and James the Less; and Sts. John the Evangelist and James the Great. The Prayer Book of Anne de Bretagne, also illustrated by Jean Poyet, includes a Suffrage (different from the one here) mentioning Anne's trio of husbands. (Feast day: July 26)

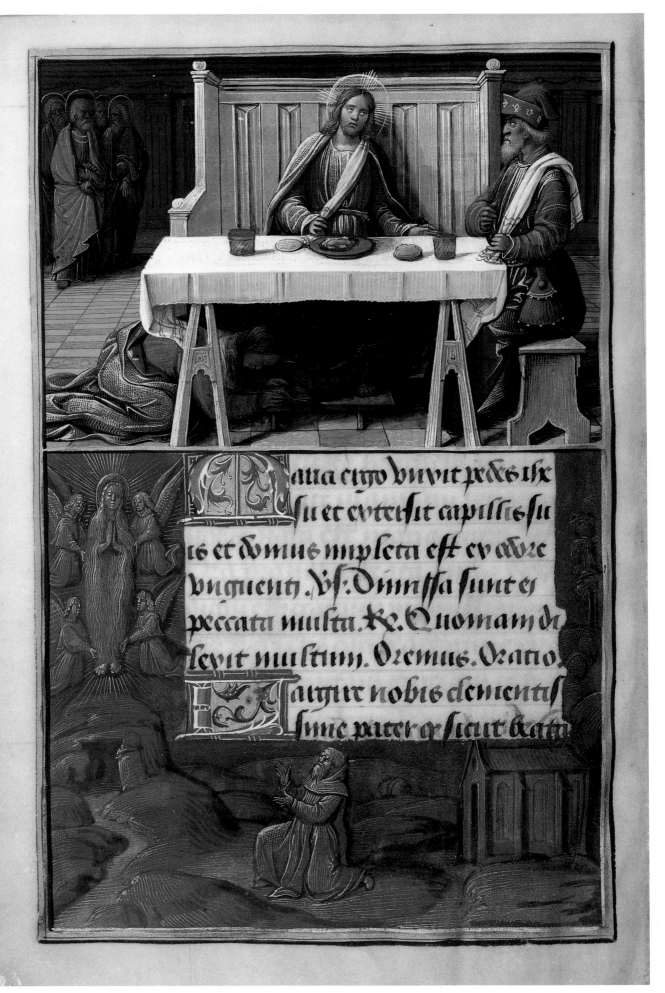

St. Mary Magdalene: Mary Magdalene Washing the Feet of Christ
border: Levitation of Mary Magdalene (fol. 187v)

The legend of Mary Magdalene, the archetypal repentant woman sinner, is a conflation of three New Testament persons: Mary of the village of Magdala from whom Jesus drove seven devils; Mary of Bethany, sister of Lazarus and Martha; and the unnamed sinner at Simon the Pharisee's (or Leper's) house who washed Christ's feet with her tears and then anointed them. Be that as it may, Mary Magdalene witnessed Christ's Crucifixion, prepared his body for burial, and was the first witness to his Resurrection.

In the miniature of Christ's dinner at Simon's house, the Magdalene dries Christ's feet with her long, flowing hair while the Savior leans to the Pharisee, stiff with indignation, and defends her actions. At the left, the apostles huddle together in disapproval.

After Christ's Ascension, according to an eleventh-century Provençal legend recorded in the *Golden Legend,* Mary, with Sts. Martha and Lazarus, was cast adrift in a rudderless boat by infidels; guided by an angel, however, they reached Marseilles, France. After a period of preaching, Mary retired to the cave of Sainte-Baume in the Maritime Alps, passing thirty years in penitence and contemplation. Never eating food, she was refreshed by the songs of the heavenly hosts, which she heard when angels carried her aloft every day at the canonical Hours. On one occasion, a hermit, who had built a cell near the Magdalene's grotto, witnessed the angels lifting and returning the saint to earth. Wanting proof of what he had seen, he ran to where she appeared, but was paralyzed and could not approach farther. The saint then revealed her identity.

The immobilized hermit witnessing Mary's celestial feeding is shown in the border. The iconography of her ascension via angels, begun in the twelfth century, is based on the Assumption of the Virgin. The Magdalene's hair, which has grown down to her feet, covers her body. (Feast day: July 22)

Virgo sancta katherina egirae gemma vrbe ale
xandrina costi regis erat filia. Vs
Diffusa est gratia in labijs tuis.
R. Propterea benedixit te deus te
eus qui Oro. terciui.
dedisti legem moysi in lu

St. Catherine: Catherine Rescued from the Torture Wheels border: Decapitation of Catherine (fol. 188v)

According to the *Golden Legend,* Catherine was the daughter of King Costas of Cyprus. Renowned for her noble birth and education, she attracted the interest of the early fourth-century Emperor Maxentius (r. 306–12) who wanted to marry her. She refused him, having chosen instead to become the "bride of Christ."

Believing he could force the young woman to apostatize, Maxentius gathered fifty prominent pagan philosophers in Alexandria to convince her of the errors of Christianity. Catherine successfully refuted them and even converted the philosophers, who were subsequently executed. Catherine, however, was unharmed as Maxentius still lusted after her. Her steadfast refusal of the emperor led to the order for execution. Two spiked wheels, which were to grind against each other, were constructed and the saint was placed between them. She prayed to the Lord for the machine to fall to pieces so that his name would be praised and that those who stood by might be converted. Instantly an angel struck the device with such violence it broke apart, killing her tormentors.

In frustration, Maxentius ordered the saint beheaded, the subject depicted in the margin. The emperor, holding a staff, looks on as the executioner prepares to do his job (his sword is hidden by the text).

At her death, Catherine prayed to Jesus that "whosoever shall celebrate the memory of my passion, or shall call upon me at the moment of death or in any necessity, may obtain the benefit of thy mercy," increasing the popularity of her cult and ensuring the efficacy of her intercession. After her death, angels carried the body of Catherine to Mount Sinai, where it is still preserved in the famous monastery that bears her name. (Feast day: formerly November 25)

St. Margaret: Margaret and Olybrius
border: Margaret and the Dragon (fol. 189v)

Margaret was the daughter of Theodosius of Antioch, a third-century pagan prince. Shortly after her birth, Margaret's mother died, so her father placed his daughter in the care of a countrywoman, a secret Christian, who raised the young girl in that faith. Later, after Margaret's conversion was discovered, she was disowned and banished with her nurse from the palace. They lived in the country as shepherdesses. One day Governor Olybrius of Antioch, as in the miniature, saw Margaret spinning wool while tending sheep and fell in love with her. Margaret's refusal to yield her faith angered Olybrius; he ordered her tortured and thrown into prison, where a fierce dragon appeared and swallowed her. The saint made the sign of the Cross, causing the dragon to explode, freeing her from its belly. Margaret then prayed that women in labor invoking her name would be as safely delivered as she was from the dragon.

During the late fourteenth and early fifteenth centuries, Margaret was most frequently shown guarding sheep; later, the prison scene with the dragon (her primary attribute) became popular. (Feast day: formerly July 20)

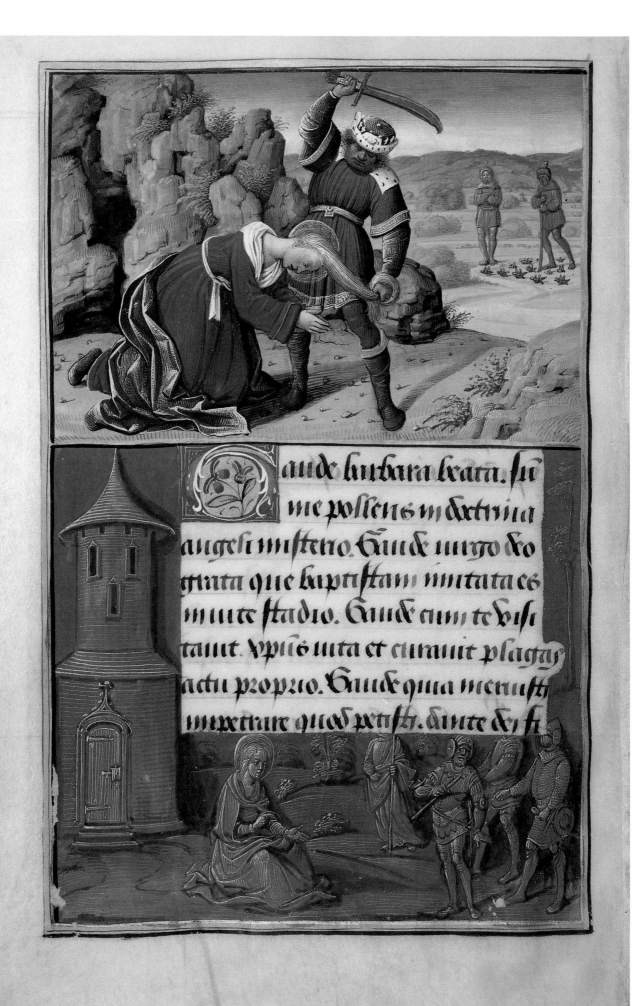

aude barbara beata. fir
me pollens in doctrina
angeli misterio. Gaude virgo do
ctrinata que baptistam imitata es
in uite stadio. Gaude cum te bisi
tauit. ypsis uita et curauit plagas
actu proprio. Gaude quia meruisti
impetrare quod petisti. ante dei fi

St. Barbara: Decapitation of Barbara
border: Barbara before her Tower (fol. 190v)

Legend has it that Barbara was the daughter of an Eastern governor, Dioscurus of Heliopolis, who shut her up in a two-windowed tower so that no man could see her. Seeking religious fulfillment she wrote to the Church Father Origen (c. 185–c. 254), who sent his disciple Valentine to instruct her. Disguised as her doctor, he gained access and eventually baptized her. When her father was away on a trip, Barbara had workmen add a third window—in honor of the Trinity—in her tower. Upon his return, as shown in the border, she told her father that the three windows symbolized the Father, Son, and Holy Spirit, who had illuminated her. Furious, he forced her to take refuge at the top of her tower, from which angels carried her away to a secret hiding place. Two shepherds who saw her fly up to a mountain where they kept their sheep betrayed her. Dioscurus handed his daughter over to the Proconsul Marcian for torture, but she steadfastly refused to renounce Christianity. Out of anger and frustration, Dioscurus dragged his daughter by the hair to the mountaintop and cut off her head, as shown in the miniature. In the rocks behind is the cave where she hid, while at the right are the two shepherds who betrayed her, their flock of sheep, through divine retribution, transformed into insects at their feet. (Feast day: formerly December 4)

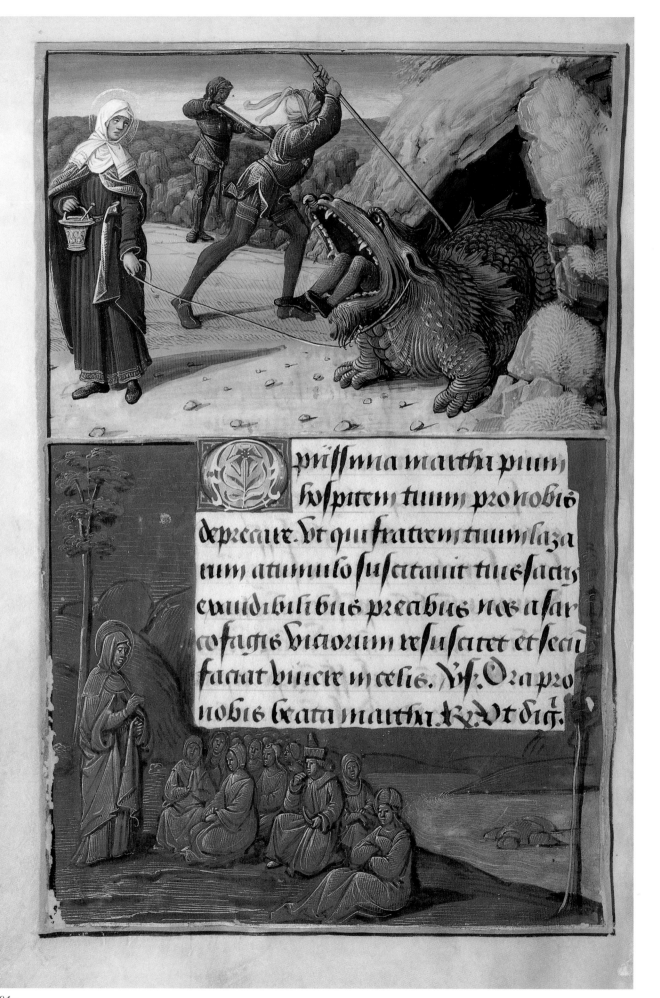

Opuissima martha pium
hospitem tuum pro nobis
deprecare. Vt qui fratrem tuum laza
rum a tumulo suscitauit tu e sacris
euandibili bus precibus nos a sar
cofagis vitaorum resuscitet et secu
faciat viuere in celis. Vs. Ora pro
nobis beata martha. R. Vt dig.

St. Martha: Martha Taming the Tarasque
border: Martha Preaching (fol. 191v)

Martha was the sister of Lazarus and Mary Magdalene (see p. 167). After Christ's Ascension, they were set adrift in a boat, which was guided by an angel to Marseilles. There, according to legend, Martha overcame a dragon, the Tarasque, which had been terrorizing the people of Tarascon in Provence. Half-animal and half-fish, the monster slew passersby and sank ships. The people appealed to Martha for help. Armed with an aspergillum (a device to sprinkle holy water) and holy water bucket she went after the dragon, which she found devouring a man. After subduing the beast with holy water, as in the miniature, she bound it about the neck with her girdle and led it away to be killed. One man plunges a spear into its neck while another—at a considerably safer distance—aims his crossbow.

Martha, devoting herself to prayer and fasting, remained in Tarascon, where a great community of religious women grew up around her. One day, while she was preaching on the bank of the Rhône River near Avignon her second famous miracle occurred. A young man on the opposite bank was eager to hear her words. Having no boat, he attempted to swim across, but he was overcome by the current and drowned (as shown in the border). After the body was recovered, it was laid at the saint's feet so that she might revive him. In her prayer she asked Christ, who had raised her brother Lazarus to life, to do the same for the dead youth. Taking the young man by the hand, she caused him to rise at once, and he was baptized. (Feast day: July 29)

All Saints: All Male Saints
border: All Female Saints (fol. 192v)

All Saints was a catchall feast of Eastern origin, which celebrated the "martyrs of the whole world" on the first Sunday after Pentecost. (In the early Church all saints, with the exception of the apostles, were martyrs.) During the last few years (c. 303–05) of Emperor Diocletian's reign so many Christians were martyred that it became impossible for each to have his or her own assigned day for commemoration, hence this all-encompassing feast. With the dedication of the Pantheon in Rome to St. Mary of the Martyrs on 13 May 609 (or 610), the feast changed to that date. When Pope Gregory III dedicated a chapel on November 1 to All Saints in St. Peter's Basilica, the feast was changed to that day, where it has remained. According to the *Golden Legend,* the date was changed so that greater crowds could come to Rome after the harvest and vintage to participate in the popular celebration. In English the feast is known as All Hallows and the night before as Hallowe'en (short for All Saints' Eve).

Within the context of Suffrages in a Book of Hours, this massive grouping of saints serves an additional purpose. By praying to all the saints at once, they might join in their intercession. Surely, it would be impossible for God not to grant the prayers of all the saints on one's behalf. Little wonder that the feast day was such a favorite.

Images of all saints typically show them in ranks. In accordance with a well established hierarchy, the male saints outranked the females (hence the women's relegation to the margin). The male saints were further ordered by status: first came the apostles, followed by martyrs, and then confessors. Poyet suggests these divisions by placing Peter and Paul at the head of the contingent. Close behind them are the four evangelists; the young man at left dressed in white is John, the beloved disciple. Behind them the rest of the saints form an isocephalic horizon. The women below, seated with books or praying, have no identifying attributes. (Feast day: November 1)

APPENDICES

A. Description of the Manuscript

Hours of Henry VIII

New York, Pierpont Morgan Library, MS H.8

    France, Tours, c. 1500

    Vellum, 200 leaves, 25.7 x 18 (text area: 15.7 x 9.5) cm, 1 column, 17 lines, in Latin and French, written in *bâtarde* script (by the same scribe who wrote the *Chronique martinienne* in Copenhagen, Kongelige Bibliotek, MS Thott 430 2°), 14 large and 29 half-page miniatures, and 12 Calendar illustrations, illuminated by Jean Poyet and his workshop.

    Use: Calendar: Franciscan, with some Parisian elements; Hours of the Virgin: Rome; Office of the Dead: Rome.

Text	Image
CALENDAR (1–6v)	Zodiacal sign on each recto and verso; each monochrome border is filled with specific or generic saints or events commemorated in the calendar
January	Feasting and Keeping Warm (1)
February	Keeping Warm (1v)
March	Pruning (2)
April	Picking Flowers and Making Wreaths (2v)
May	Picking Branches (3)
June	Mowing (3v)
July	Reaping (4)
August	Threshing (4v)
September	Treading Grapes (5)
October	Sowing and Ploughing (5v)
November	Thrashing for Acorns (6)
December	Roasting Slaughtered Pigs (6v)
GOSPEL LESSONS (7–12v)	
John	John on Patmos; border: John Boiled in Oil (7)
Luke	Luke Writing; border: Annunciation (9)
Matthew	Matthew Writing; border: Magi Meeting at the Crossroads (10v)
Mark	Mark Contemplating; border: Christ Preaching to a Crowd (12)
PASSION ACCORDING TO JOHN (13–21v)	*"Ego sum"* (13)
PRAYERS TO THE VIRGIN (21v–29v)	
"Obsecro te"	Holy Family; border: Musical Angels (21v)
"O intemerata"	(miniature probably missing between 23/24)
"Stabat mater"	Lamentation; border: Deposition (26)

Text	Image
Mass of the Virgin	(miniature probably missing between 27/28)
(blank, 30)	
HOURS OF THE VIRGIN (31–93v)	
Matins	Annunciation (30v)
Lauds	Visitation (40v)
Prime	Nativity (51v)
Terce	Annunciation to the Shepherds (56v)
Sext	Adoration of the Magi (61v)
None	Presentation in the Temple (65v)
Vespers	Massacre of the Innocents and Flight into Egypt (69v)
Compline	(miniature missing between 73/74)
HOURS OF THE CROSS (94–101)	Christ Carrying the Cross (94v)
HOURS OF THE HOLY SPIRIT (102–106v)	Pentecost (101v)
(blank, 107)	
PENITENTIAL PSALMS AND LITANY (107v–127)	David and Uriah (108v)
OFFICE OF THE DEAD (127–167v)	
Vespers	Job on the Dungheap (127v)
Matins and Lauds	Feast of Dives; border: Dives in Hell (134v)
SEVEN PRAYERS OF ST. GREGORY (168v–169v)	Mass of St. Gregory (168)
SUFFRAGES (170v–193)	
St. Jerome	Jerome in Penance (170)
The Trinity	Trinity; border: Angels (171)
St. Michael the Archangel	Michael Battling a Devil; border: Fall of the Rebel Angels (172)
St. John the Baptist	Baptism of Christ; border: John the Baptist Preaching (173)
St. John the Evangelist	John the Evangelist Descending into His Grave; border: John and the Beast of the Apocalypse (174)
Sts. Peter and Paul	Fall of Simon Magus; border: Decapitation of Paul and Crucifixion of Peter (175)
St. James	James with Hermogenes; border: Decapitation of James (176)
St. Philip	Philip Vanquishing Idols and a Demon; border: Philip Baptizing (177)
St. Christopher	Conversion of Christopher; border: Christopher Carrying Christ (178)
St. Sebastian	Sebastian Shot with Arrows, Abandoned by Archers; border: Sebastian's Body Cast into the Sewer (179)
St. Claude of Besançon	Claude Resuscitating a Dead Man; border: Pilgrims Kneeling before Claude's Shrine (180v)
St. Adrian	Martyrdom of Adrian; border: Christians in Prison (181v)

Text	Image
St. Nicholas	Nicholas Giving Gold to the Three Maidens; border: Nicholas Resuscitating the Three Boys (182v)
St. Anthony	Temptation of Anthony; border: Anthony in the Wilderness (183v)
St. Francis	Stigmatization of Francis; border: Francis in the Fiery Chariot (184v)
St. Anthony of Padua	Anthony and the Miracle of the Kneeling Horse; border: Anthony Preaching (185v)
St. Anne	Anne Instructing the Virgin; border: Presentation of the Virgin in the Temple (186v)
St. Mary Magdalene	Mary Magdalene Washing the Feet of Christ; border: Levitation of Mary Magdalene (187v)
St. Catherine	Catherine Rescued from the Torture Wheels; border: Decapitation of Catherine (188v)
St. Margaret	Margaret and Olybrius; border: Margaret and the Dragon (189v)
St. Barbara	Decapitation of Barbara; border: Barbara before her Tower (190v)
St. Martha	Martha Taming the Tarasque; border: Martha Preaching (191v)
All Saints	All Male Saints; border: All Female Saints (192v)
(blank, 193v)	

SERIES OF PRAYERS (194–199v)

When waking up *("In matutinis Domine meditabor in te . . . Gratias ago tibi Domine omnipotens eterne Deus qui me in hac nocte. . . .");*

When leaving the house *("Vias tuas Domine demonstra michi. . . .");*

When entering the church *("Asperges me Domine ysopo. . . .");*

Before a crucifix *("Salva nos Xriste salvator per virtutem sancte crucis. . . . Crucem tuam adoramus et veneramur. . . .");*

When the priest turns to the people [during Mass at the *"Orate fratres"*] *("Spiritus sancti gratia illustret et illuminet cor. . . .");*

At the Elevation of the Host *("Anima Xristi sanctifica me. Corpus Xristi salva me. . . .");*

At the Elevation of the Chalice *("Ave
vere sanguis Domini Nostri
Ihesu Xristi. . . .");*
Athanasian Creed *("Quicumque* [sic] *vult
salvus esse. . . .").*

PROVENANCE NOTE BY GEORGE WADE (200)

(blank, 200v)

Collation

As the collation diagram below indicates, all of the gatherings have eight leaves except for I (6), IV (7), X (6), XVIII (6), XXII (6), XXV (10), XXVI (7). In Books of Hours the first gathering, containing the Calendar, often has six leaves, one page for each of the twelve months. Of the other six odd gatherings only two have missing texts or missing miniatures. In gathering IV, a missing leaf between folios 23 and 24 contained the end of the *"Obsecro te"* and the beginning of the *"O intemerata,"* as well as the miniature that preceded the latter; the missing conjoint leaf, between folios 27 and 28, contained the end of the *"Stabat mater"* and (most probably) a miniature for the Mass of the Virgin. Folio 29 is a tabbed-in leaf (there is no textual break between fols. 22 and 23). In gathering X a bifolio is also missing: the leaf between folios 71 and 72 contained part of Vespers, while that between folios 73 and 74 contained the end of Vespers and the full-page miniature for Compline (probably a Coronation of the Virgin). Only two partly trimmed catchwords remain (fols. 29v, 37v); the others were removed during a rebinding.

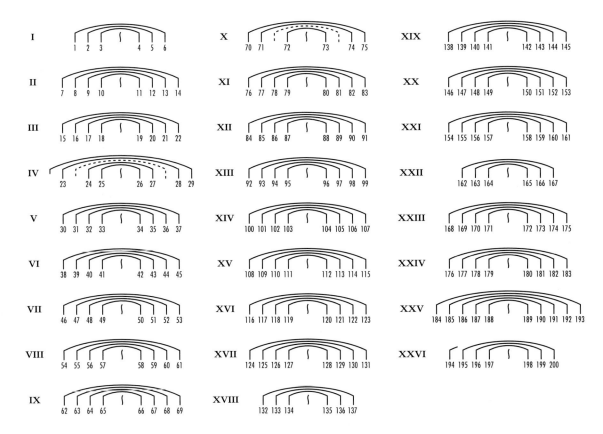

182

Although the original owner of the Hours of Henry VIII is not known—there are no contemporaneous portraits, coats of arms, heraldic devices, or inscriptions—the book must have been commissioned by a person of considerable wealth and social position, probably someone connected with the French court or a member of the royal family. We are, however, much better informed about the later history of the book, thanks to a note supplied by George Wade on its last blank leaf (fol. 200; fig. 44):

> *In the Year 1723, being at Mons and hearing of This Book as the greatest Curiosity of its kind, I found it in the hands of Mons[ieu]r Charle Benoit Desmanet, a Gent[lema]n of that Town, (and after his Death procured it from his Executors) he Shew'd it me with great care and precaution not Suffering me to touch it, but turn'd over the leaves with a Small pair of Silver Tongues made for that purpose, And perceiving me to Smile at this Nicety, he said with some Warmth, Sir In this manner my Ancestors for above a hundred Years past have preserved this Book from blemish and in the Perfection you now see it; He told me likewise That the Tradition of the Family was That it was formerly A Present from the Emperor Charles the Fifth to Henry the Eighth King of England, and that after his Death it was taken out of his Closet and brought into Flanders; The Painter is Unknown;*
>
> *George Wade.*

George Wade (1673–1748) was a field marshal, the highest-ranking military officer in the British army; he received that honor in 1743, when he was also appointed commander-in-chief of the British forces in Flanders. He was certainly suited for the latter position because of his prior service there, which had already begun in 1702, at the siege of Liège and elsewhere. Wade apparently heard about

Fig. 44. George Wade, provenance note, from the "Hours of Henry VIII"; ?England, London, between 1723 and 1740. New York, Pierpont Morgan Library, MS H.8, fol. 200.

the manuscript in 1723, as the note tells us, when he was in Mons, and successfully tracked down its owner, a certain Charle Benoit Desmanet. Because of his trips to the Lowlands he was able to keep his eye on the manuscript—and Desmanet—contacting his executors after his death. Marshal Wade had a taste for art and took full advantage of his trips to Flanders; on one occasion, reported in a letter by Horace Walpole, he purchased a version of Peter Paul Ruben's *Chase of Meleager and Atalanta* that was too large for his London house, forcing him to sell it to Walpole's father! Wade was evidently impressed with the manuscript's connection with Henry VIII and recognized the potential opportunities that its possession might bring. Whether he sold or gave the manuscript directly to King George II of

England has not been established. By 1740, however, a few years before he was named field marshal, the manuscript was already in the hands of the king, for in that year he presented it to his Royal Library in Hanover, where a special box in which it was kept bore the label "Donum regium 1740" (Gift of the King 1740). The present red velvet binding and silver clasps (fig. 45) were already on the manuscript when it entered the Royal Library, for they are mentioned in a 17 June 1740 note by Gruber, the then director. The manuscript had been transferred to Gruber by the Cabinet-Secretary of the Realm (Hanover, Niedersächsische Landesbibliothek, Akten V 15). The note, however, does not specifically mention that the clasps contain Henry VIII's coat of arms (they are the Royal arms: three fleurs-de-lis quarterly 1 and 4, three lions passant guardant quarterly 2 and 4); monogram, "H.8.R." (Henricus Octavus Rex); and motto, HONI SOIT QUI MAL Y PENSE (Shame on him who evil thinks). The manuscript was further embellished with contemporaneous so-called Dutch Gilt endpapers (of German manufacture) and paper flyleaves bearing a watermark with the name of Villedary.

Desmanet's assertion that the manuscript was a gift of Charles V (ruled as Holy Roman Emperor, 1519–56) was repeated until the twentieth century, when it was dismissed on the grounds that the emperor would never have ordered a book in France. The ownership of Henry VIII (r. 1509–47)—since he was too young to have commissioned the book himself—was then explained by Paul Vitry as a gift from Francis I (r. 1515–47), on the occasion of their meeting in 1520 on the Field

Fig. 45. Silver clasp, from the "Hours of Henry VIII"; second quarter of the eighteenth century. New York, Pierpont Morgan Library, MS H.8, top clasp.

of the Cloth of Gold. The idea seemed to fit in very well with a payment record of 10 March 1518 for a *"Grandes Heures"* commissioned by Francis I. There are two major problems with this identification, however; the Hours of Henry VIII actually dates much earlier (about 1500), and the payment was to Jean Bourdichon, who had provided decorations for the meeting and to whom the manuscript cannot be attributed. (Léopold Delisle's observation that the manuscript was by the same scribe as the *Grandes Heures* of Anne de Bretagne further fueled the mistaken attribution.)

It is certain, however, that Henry VIII owned at least one manuscript illuminated by Poyet, the Hours of Mary of England (see pp. 26–27). Mary Tudor, Henry's sister, had received that manuscript from King Louis XII during her short-lived marriage to him in 1514; after Louis's death on 1 January 1515, she returned to England, taking the book with her. According to an inscription in the manuscript, she subsequently gave it to her brother. While it is possible that she brought the Hours of Henry VIII back with her as well, or that Henry VIII once owned the manuscript (old traditions, though not always completely accurate, may contain some element of truth), there is no supporting evidence found in the manuscript itself. An earlier rebinding of the manuscript may have resulted in the loss of telltale inventory numbers or other inscriptions, as well as three miniatures (which, it must be admitted, could have contained heraldic material pointing to another owner). The two miniatures were not included in the seventeenth- or early eighteenth-century three-page description attached to the second flyleaf at the beginning of the manuscript. In any case, because of the traditional association with Henry VIII, the manuscript became known as the "Great Hours of Henry VIII," or, more simply, the "Hours of Henry VIII."

King George II (1683–1760) was the second of the Hanoverian line of kings of England. George I (George Louis: 1660–1727), the great-grandson of James I of England, was the elector of Hanover (in Germany) who, through the British Act of

Settlement, succeeded Queen Anne as king of Great Britain and Ireland. He spoke no English, favored two German mistresses, and was the first British monarch of the House of Brunswick (r. 1714–27). George II (George Augustus), who reigned from 1727 to 1760 and was the last British king to lead his troops in battle (at Dettingen, 1743), was nevertheless devoted to his ancestral Hanover, where he maintained a large library. Indeed, a number of visitors saw the Hours of Henry VIII there and recorded their impressions. Stephan Halmágyi (1719–1785), of Siebenbürgen (the German name of Transylvania), for example, included in his diary a detailed account of his visit to the Royal Library on 24 October 1752 (Christian Scheidt, the historian and librarian, showed him around). His entry, the longest for any object in the library, described the manuscript as a Missal and repeated the story that it was given by Charles V to Henry VIII.

On every second or third page were represented stories of the Old and New Testament; there were pictures of the saints and their miracles, all executed with so much art, with such vivacity of color, and with such careful realization of details, as if they had been painted today. I could not imagine if anyone now could paint so many perfect images as those which I have seen. Among others was pictured how our Lord Jesus Christ, still a child, was held in the arms, and presented for the first time in the Temple [fol. 65v]. Already, at the time, a Benedictine monk was present. I do not know where the manuscript originated. My impression is that it came from a London library, and that the English would not take kindly to that fact if they knew it.

J. Meermann, Freiherr von Dalem, in his travel publication of 1793, also spoke of his visit to the library, describing the manuscript (which he called a Breviary) as a rarity; its miniatures, he said, "were the finest of their kind, and he had never seen any that approached them in drawing, expression, color, and gold." The silver tongs mentioned by Wade were still preserved with the manuscript.

After the death of George II, the manuscript passed to his son George III (George William Frederick: 1738–1820), who reigned from 1760 to 1820. Although it was this king who lost the American colonies, he took special precautions to ensure that his valuable possessions in Hanover did not meet a similar fate during the Napoleonic invasions of Germany. In 1803, these possessions (including the Hours of Henry VIII) were recalled to England for safekeeping.

In 1816, six years after George III became permanently insane, the manuscript was returned to Hanover, where it remained under George IV (George Augustus Frederick: 1762–1830; r. 1820–30) and then his brother, William IV (William Henry: 1765–1837; r. 1830–37). When William's niece, Queen Victoria (r. 1837–1901), ascended the throne, however, Hanover separated from the British Crown (the Salic law of succession barred women), bringing to an end the 123-year-old union between the two kingdoms. Consequently the manuscript became the property of Ernest Augustus (duke of Cumberland and fifth son of George III), who then became the king of Hanover; when he died in 1851, he was succeeded by his son, George V (Frederick Alexander Karl Ernest Augustus, 1819–1878), who had founded the Guelph Museum in 1861. In the same year George V purchased the celebrated Gospels of Henry the Lion, the fate of which would become inextricably linked with the Hours of Henry VIII. The former, which George V never saw (he was totally blind by 1833), is the uncontested masterpiece of the Helmarshausen school of illumination; it was made by the monk Herimann about 1173–75. (The Gospels of Henry the Lion, until recently, was the most expensive medieval manuscript sold at auction; it brought $11.8 million at Sotheby's in London on 6 December 1983, lot 50.) Henry the Lion (1129/30–1195), duke of Saxony and Bavaria, had granted Hanover its municipal charter; he was George V's most prestigious ancestor, and the acquisition of his manuscript carried with it no little symbolism. The Gospels of Henry the Lion was for a time loaned to the Guelph Museum, and a special wooden box with double locks was made for it. The keys were held by Senator Friedrich Culemann (1811–1866), a discerning collector who regarded it as the "pearl in the crown of Hanover"; he suggested on 10 July 1861 that the Hours of Henry VIII should also be incorporated into the museum, and on 20 July 1861 it was placed on temporary deposit.

In 1867, however, Hanover was annexed by Prussia and George V was deposed. (Henry the Lion had also had connections with England—in 1168 he had married Matilda, the daughter of King Henry II—and had also been exiled from Hanover for a while, losing many possessions.) Deposed King George V and his family went into exile but were able to take the contents of the Guelph Museum (which was officially recognized as his property) with them. Already in late 1866 the two manuscripts had to be recalled from Culemann and removed to Marienburg, south of Hanover, where Queen Marie had gone after the occupation of Hanover. After more Prussian pressure she fled to Hietzing near Vienna; the manuscripts followed by train. In Hietzing, on 18 February 1868, joined by George V, they celebrated their silver wedding anniversary. On that occasion George movingly addressed a crowd of some two thousand Hanoverians and seventy officers, recalling how Henry the Lion also had to flee his land; just as Henry returned to an even more glorious Guelph Kingdom, he, too, hoped to return as king of Hanover. In 1869, the former king, now known as the duke of Cumberland (an English title his father had before becoming king of Hanover in 1837), placed the contents of the Guelph Museum on display at the Museum of Art and Industry in Vienna, where they remained until 1906. The two manuscripts, however, were not included; they were kept at the so-called Lothringer-Haus in Penzing until 1895, when they were put under the jurisdiction of a Guelph Foundation. The deposed royal couple retired to Cumberland Castle, a neo-Gothic structure in Gmunden, Austria, situated midway between Salzburg and Linz. After George's death in 1878, the manuscripts passed to his son, Duke Ernest Augustus I (1845–1923), who, in 1906, had them delivered to Cumberland Castle (hence the other popular name by which the Hours of Henry VIII was known, the Cumberland Hours), where they were placed under the guardianship of Heinrich Buck, the librarian. Duke Ernest Augustus I became duke of Brunswick in 1884, but renounced his rights to that duchy on 24 October 1913 in favor of his son, Duke Ernest Augustus II (1887–1953). Among the latter's many titles was that of Grand Master of the Order of Henry the Lion (granted 1 November 1913).

It was Duke Ernest Augustus II—he preferred to be called the prince of Hanover—who was to sell the Guelph Treasure and the two manuscripts. Each manuscript was offered twice to the Morgan Library, but not purchased; the Gospels of Henry the Lion in 1933 and 1949, and the Hours of Henry the VIII in 1923 and 1933. In 1923, according to a document in the Hauptstaatsarchiv Hannover (Hausarchiv S. K. H. des Prinzen Ernst August von Hannover, Dep. 103 XXI Nr. 719), the Hours of Henry VIII was sold for a discounted price of £7,275 (then about $32,000) to an otherwise unidentified person named Eisenmann. (Perhaps this was Heinrich Eisemann, a Frankfurt book dealer who emigrated to London in the mid-1930s; he was known in the trade as a ten percent man, acting primarily as a commission agent for collectors.) In the same year Joseph Baer & Co., the Frankfurt rare book firm, sent Belle da Costa Greene (the librarian of John Pierpont Morgan, Jr.) a copy of the privately printed *Description of the Great Book of Hours of Henry the Eighth Illuminated by Jean Bourdichon of Tours* (n.p., 1923), which included fifty-five heliotype reproductions of all its miniatures. According to a note by Belle Greene, which was subsequently placed in the Library's copy of the publication, she questioned both Henry VIII's ownership and the attribution to Bourdichon, suggesting instead his pupil or school. The manuscript had been consigned (by Eisenmann?) to Baer, who, in a cable to the Library (20 December 1923), offered it for $90,000. Belle Greene simply annotated the cable with the word "Refused." By 1930 the manuscript was purchased by Baer and offered in the firm's monumental catalogue no. 750 *(One Thousand Fine & Valuable Books, Manuscripts, Drawings, Prints, and Autograph Letters),* where it was item 805 and illustrated with five plates. No price was given, but in a letter Baer wrote to Belle Greene (23 October 1930), it had been lowered to $55,000. In spite of Raimond van Marle's letter to Belle Greene (29 November 1933) regarding the importance of the manuscript, she remained unconvinced. Shortly thereafter the manuscript was purchased by Dannie H. Heineman (1872–1962), as a gift for his wife, Hettie. (According to the note Belle Greene added to the Baer letter, the book was sold through Graupe at the Carlisle Hotel in New York for less than half the price at which it was offered to the Morgan Library. The agent was undoubtedly Paul Graupe, who had apprenticed before World War I with Martin Breslauer, the head of the distinguished Berlin book firm.) Although Dannie Heineman was born in Charlotte, North Carolina, he had spent some fifty years in Brussels as the head of the Belgian company SOFINA. His mother, however, was German, and though he wished to study medicine, he took a degree in electrical engineering (for which a scholarship was available) at the Technische Hochschule in Hanover in 1895. The school was in the former Welfenschloss (built 1857–66) and thus the provenance and the historic connections of the manuscript would have had a special appeal to him. In late 1939, the Heinemans, with their rare books and manuscripts, left Brussels, before the German invasions of the following year. The books were sent via the steamer Volendam to New York, whence they went by train to Charlotte. At the end of World War II, the Heinemans settled in Greenwich, Connecticut, where they transferred most of the collection to the newly formed Heineman Foundation for Research, Educational, Charitable and Scientific Purposes, Inc. The Hours of Henry VIII, however, remained Hettie's personal property and thus was not part of the Heineman Collection that was deposited at the Morgan Library after Dannie's death in 1962. On 24 March 1964, Frederick B. Adams, Jr., director of the Morgan Library, received it as a loan to the Foundation, but on Hettie Heineman's death (4 April 1974), she willed title to the Foundation itself.

On 17 November 1977, the Heineman Foundation gave the Dannie and Hettie Heineman Collection to the Morgan Library, which was, up to then, the most important gift received since the Library's founding in 1924. In earlier Heineman inventories the manuscripts were grouped and numbered by type, and originally the Hours of Henry VIII was designated as Hn. 6 (Heineman 6). After Mrs. Heineman had added her manuscripts to the deposit, they were sequentially numbered without regard to type, and the designation of MS H.8 ensued. It is thus ironic that the manuscript, formerly owned by five kings and several dukes of Cumberland, should have received a shelf mark implying the name of Henry the Eighth. Nevertheless, his association with the manuscript—be it real or manufactured—certainly bestowed upon it a celebrity that caused it to be cherished by later kings and that is preserved to this day in its popular name and the title of the present publication.

—W.M.V.

C. Bibliographies

The bibliographies are divided into four sections: (A) Jean Poyet (arranged in four parts); (B) Books of Hours and Liturgy; (C) Saints and Iconography; and (D) Full-Citation List, which includes full citations for works abbreviated in the first three sections.

SECTION A
JEAN POYET

1. The Early Bibliography. The early bibliography on Jean Poyet is much confused because of the mistaken attribution of Anne de Bretagne's *Grandes Heures* to him. The early authors discussing Poyet's putative involvement in the *Grandes Heures* are the following: Laborde, *La Renaissance des arts à la cour de France,* 273–75; Ferdinand Denis, *Histoire de l'ornementation des manuscrits,* Paris, 1857, 119–20; Le Roux de Lincy, *Vie de la reine Anne de Bretagne, femme des rois de France Charles VIII et Louis XII, suivi des lettres inédits et des documents originaux,* 4 vols., Paris, 1860, III, 77–80; and his article, "Le livre d'heures d'Anne de Bretagne," *Gazette des beaux-arts,* 1st series, VI, 1860, 151–54; Paris, Musée national du Louvre, Département des objects d'art du Moyen Âge, de la Renaissance et des temps modernes, *Notice des antiquités objets . . . composant le musée des souverains par Henri Barbet de Jouy,* Paris, 1866, 85; and Jules Labarte (who, however, doubts the connection between Poyet and the *Grandes Heures*), *Histoire des arts industriels au Moyen Âge et à l'époque de la Renaissance,* 4 vols., Paris, 1864–66, III, 300–04.

André Steyert published the 1508 payment document linking Jean Bourdichon to the *Grandes Heures* in "Jehan Bourdichon: Prix et quittance du livre d'heures d'Anne de Bretagne, 14 Mars, 1508," *Nouvelles archives de l'art français,* 2nd series, II, 1880–81, 1–11. Still linking Poyet to the *Grandes Heures* (willfully or out of ignorance) were

the following: E. Giraudet, *Les artistes tourangeaux,* Tours, 1885, 338–39; John W. Bradley, *A Dictionary of Miniaturists, Illuminators, Calligraphers, and Copyists. . . . ,* 3 vols., London, 1887–89, III, 93–94; and the ever quarrelsome F. de Mély, "Les 'Heures d'Anne de Bretagne' et les inscriptions de leurs miniatures: Jean Bourdichon ou Jean Poyet?" *Gazette des beaux-arts,* 2nd series, II, 1909, 177–96.

Finally, among those authors who severed Poyet from the *Grandes Heures* are the following: Léopold Delisle, *Le cabinet des manuscrits de la Bibliothèque nationale. . . . ,* 4 vols., Paris, 1868–81, III, 345–47; A. Lecoy de La Marche, *Les manuscrits et la miniature,* Paris, 1884, 242; Émile Mâle, "Trois oeuvres nouvelles de Jean Bourdichon, peintre de Charles VIII, de Louis XII et de François Ier," and "Jean Bourdichon et son atelier," *Gazette des beaux-arts,* 1st series, XXVII, 1902, 185–203, and 1st series, XXXII, 1904, 441–57, respectively; L. Dimier, *French Painting in the Sixteenth Century,* London, 1904, 11–12; Henry Martin, *Les miniaturistes français,* Paris, 1906, 45, 94–95; J. A. Herbert, *Illuminated Manuscripts,* London, 1911, 284; and David MacGibbon, *Jean Bourdichon: A Court Painter of the Fifteenth Century,* Glasgow, 1933, 117–122 (who offers a minihistory of the controversy).

2. The Documents. The documents surrounding the name of Poyet can be found in the following: Charles L. Grandmaison, *Documents inédits pour servir à l'histoire des arts en Touraine,* Tours, 1870, 9–10, 10–11, and 39–40; Laborde, *La Renaissance des arts à la cour de France;* and Girault, "Jean Poyet."

3. Recent Discussion. The chief sources for the recent discussion of Poyet are the following: Plummer, *Last Flowering;* Backhouse, "Tilliot

Hours"; Backhouse, "The Tilliot Hours: Comparisons and Relationships"; Avril and Reynaud, *Manuscrits à peintures;* Girault, "Jean Poyet"; Backhouse, "Poyet, Jean"; and Wieck, *The Prayer Book of Anne de Bretagne.*

4. Bibliography for Poyet's Major Works.
What follows is a list of all the artworks—manuscripts (arranged alphabetically by city), drawings, and painting—attributed to Poyet that are discussed in chapter 2. Each entry is accompanied by the most recent bibliographic citations, from which earlier literature can often be extracted.

Manuscripts
Book of Hours
Baltimore, Walters Art Gallery, MS W.295

Plummer, *Last Flowering,* 87; Wieck, *Time Sanctified,* 61, 202, no. 67, pl. 20; Randall, *Medieval and Renaissance Manuscripts in the Walters Art Gallery,* II, 410–13, no. 185, pl. XXb, fig. 325.

Book of Hours
Baltimore, Walters Art Gallery, MS W.430

Wieck, *Time Sanctified,* 132, 202–03, no. 68, fig. 123; Randall, *Medieval and Renaissance Manuscripts in the Walters Art Gallery,* II, 440–44, no. 192, pl. XXd, figs. 338, 339; Avril and Reynaud, *Manuscrits à peintures,* 307, 314.

"Hours of Jean Lallemant the Elder"
Baltimore, Walters Art Gallery, MS W.459

See London, British Library, Add. MS 39641.

"Hours of Jean Lallemant the Elder"
Cambridge, Fitzwilliam Museum, Marlay Cutting, Fr. 7

See London, British Library, Add. MS 39641.

Chronique martinienne
Copenhagen, Kongelige Bibliotek, MS Thott 430 2°

N. C. L. Abrahams, *Description des manuscrits français du Moyen Âge de la Bibliothèque royale de Copenhagen, précédée d'une notice historique sur cette bibliothèque,* Copenhagen, 1844, 78–80, no. XXXI; Copenhagen, Nationalmuseet, *Gyldne Bøger,* 87–88, no. 178; Backhouse, "The Tilliot Hours: Comparisons and Relationships," 228; Avril and Reynaud, *Manuscrits à peintures,* 308, 313, 314; Erik Petersen, ed., *Living Words & Luminous Pictures: Medieval Book Culture in Denmark,* Copenhagen, 1999, 91, no. 128, illus.

Book of Hours
Copenhagen, Kongelige Bibliotek, MS Thott 541 4°

Ellen Jørgensen, *Catalogus codicum latinorum medii ævi Bibliothecæ Regiæ Hafniensis,* Copenhagen, 1926, 224; Copenhagen, Nationalmuseet, *Gyldne Bøger,* 88, no. 181; Avril and Reynaud, *Manuscrits à peintures,* 307, 318.

"Briçonnet Hours"
Haarlem, Teylers Museum, MS 78

Plummer, *Last Flowering,* 85, 87; Backhouse, "Tilliot Hours," 180 n. 18; Avril and Reynaud, *Manuscrits à peintures,* 306, 308, 308–10, 315, 317, no. 169, illus. For the history of the Briçonnet family, see Guy Bretonneau, *Histoire généalogique de la maison des Briçonnets,* Paris, 1621.

Book of Hours
London, British Library, Add. MS 35315

Backhouse, "The Tilliot Hours: Comparisons and Relationships," 221–22, pl. VII, fig. 10; Avril and Reynaud, *Manuscrits à peintures,* 307, 317 (twice).

Pierre Louis de Valtan, *Super qualibet dictione symboli apostolici*
London, British Library, Add. MS 35320

Plummer, *Last Flowering,* 87; Backhouse, "Pierre Sala," 174 n. 21; Backhouse, "Tilliot Hours," 176, fig. 23e; Backhouse, "The Tilliot Hours: Comparisons and Relationships," 215, 217; Avril and Reynaud, *Manuscrits à peintures,* 307; Backhouse, "Poyet, Jean," 405.

"Hours of Jean Lallemant the Elder"
London, British Library, Add. MS 39641 (41 fols.);

Baltimore, Walters Art Gallery, MS W.459 (33 fols.); and

Cambridge, Fitzwilliam Museum, Marlay Cutting, Fr. 7 (single leaf)

Plummer, *Last Flowering,* 87 (as ex-Firmin-Didot); Backhouse, "Tilliot Hours," 179, fig. 23f; Backhouse, "The Tilliot Hours: Comparisons and Relationships," 215–17, 226, fig. 5; Randall, *Medieval and Renaissance Manuscripts in the Walters Art Gallery,* II, 501–09, no. 206, fig. 366; Avril and Reynaud, *Manuscrits à peintures,* 307, 312–13, no. 171, illus.

"Tilliot Hours"
London, British Library, Yates Thompson MS 5

Plummer, *Last Flowering,* 87; Backhouse, "Tilliot Hours"; Backhouse, "The Tilliot Hours: Comparisons and Relationships"; Avril and Reynaud, *Manuscrits à peintures,* 307, 309, 314 (twice), 315, 318; Backhouse, "Poyet, Jean," 405.

"Hours of Mary of England"
Lyons, Bibliothèque Municipale, MS 1558

Plummer, *Last Flowering,* 87; Backhouse, "Tilliot Hours," 179; Backhouse, "The Tilliot Hours: Comparisons and Relationships," 229–30 n. 12; Avril and Reynaud, *Manuscrits à peintures,* 307 (twice), 314–15, 318, no. 173, illus.

"Hours of Henry VIII"
New York, Pierpont Morgan Library, MS H.8

Paul Binder, with Hans Immel and Wilhelm Totok, "Das Tagebuch des Siebenbürgers Stephan Halmágyi über seine Reise nach Deutschland in den Jahren 1752/1753 unter besonderer Berücksichtigung Hannovers und seiner königlichen Bibliothek," *Niedersächsisches Jahrbuch für Landesgeschichte,* XLVI/XLVII, 1975, 31, 49 n. 89 [article = 23–57]; Plummer, *Last Flowering,* 87, 87–88, 100, no. 113, fig. 113; Backhouse, "Tilliot Hours," 179, 180 n. 15, figs. 23b, 23g; Georg Schnath, "Besitzgeschichte des Helmarshausener Evangeliars Heinrichs des Löwen (1188–1935)," *Wolfenbütteler Beiträge,* VII, 1987, 218, 225–31

[article = 179–265]; Backhouse, "The Tilliot Hours: Comparisons and Relationships," 213–14, 215, 217, 223, 224, 225–26, 227, 228, figs. 2, 3; Wieck, *Time Sanctified,* 117, 203–04, no. 70, fig. 96; Klaus Jaitner, "Die Besitzgeschichte des Evangeliars seit dem 14. Jahrhundert," in *Das Evangeliar Heinrichs des Löwen Kommentar zum Faksimile,* Dietrich Kötzsche, ed., Frankfurt, 1989, 310–12 [article = 307–15]; Avril and Reynaud, *Manuscrits à peintures,* 307, 314, 315, 318 (thrice); Backhouse, "Poyet, Jean," 405, illus.; Wieck, *Painted Prayers,* 58, no. 39, illus.

Book of Hours
New York, Pierpont Morgan Library, MS M.9

Plummer, *Last Flowering,* 87, 89.

"Prayer Book of Anne de Bretagne"
New York, Pierpont Morgan Library, MS M.50

A. Richard, "Livre de prières attribué à Anne de Bretagne," *Bibliothèque de l'École des Chartes,* XXXVIII, 1877, 389–93; F. de Mély, *Les primitifs et leurs signatures: Les miniaturistes,* Paris, 1913, 311, pl. XX, fig. 4; Paris, Théophile Belin Libraire, *Les patenostres de la reine Anne de Bretagne,* Paris [1903] (after Morgan's purchase of the manuscript in 1905, Belin reissued this booklet with a new title-page, *Les patenostres de la reine Anne de Bretagne: Manuscrit sur vélin du XVe siècle faisant partie de la bibliothèque Morgan à New York;* the text is thought to have been written by G. Pawlowski, Firmin-Didot's librarian); Belle Da Costa Greene and Meta P. Harrsen, *The Pierpont Morgan Library: Exhibition of Illuminated Manuscripts Held at the New York Public Library,* introd. by Charles Rufus Morey, New York, 1934, 55–56, no. 118, pl. 82; Seymour de Ricci, assisted by W. J. Wilson, *Census of Medieval and Renaissance Manuscripts in the United States and Canada,* New York, 1937, II, 1375, no. 50; John Plummer, with Anselm Strittmatter, *Liturgical Manuscripts for the Mass and the Divine Office,* New York, 1964, 49–50, no. 66; John Harthan, *The Book of Hours, with a Historical Survey and*

Commentary, New York, 1977, 133; Michael Jones, "Les manuscrits d'Anne de Bretagne, reine de France, duchesse de Bretagne," *Mémoires de la société d'histoire et d'archéologie de Bretagne,* LV/6, 1978, 53, 73, no. 6 [article = 43–81]; Plummer, *Last Flowering,* 87, 88–89, no. 114, fig. 114; Wilma Fitzgerald, *Ocelli nominum: Names and Shelf Marks of Famous/Familiar Manuscripts,* Toronto, 1992, 12; Avril and Reynaud, *Manuscrits à peintures,* 307, 314, 318; Wieck, *The Prayer Book of Anne de Bretagne.*

Book of Hours
New York, Pierpont Morgan Library, MS M.250
    Robert W. Scheller, "Imperial Themes in Art and Literature of the Early French Renaissance: The Period of Charles VIII," *Simiolus,* XII, 1981–82, 22–25, fig. 3 [article = 5–69]; Plummer, *Last Flowering,* 85–86, 87, no. 111, figs. 111a, 111b; Avril and Reynaud, *Manuscrits à peintures,* 307, 311–12, no. 170, illus.; Wieck, *Painted Prayers,* 17, no. 7, illus.

Book of Hours
New York, Pierpont Morgan Library, MS M.388
    Plummer, *Last Flowering,* 87, 89, no. 115, fig. 115; Avril and Reynaud, *Manuscrits à peintures,* 308, 313.

"Missal of Guillaume Lallemant"
New York, Pierpont Morgan Library, MS M.495
    Plummer, *Last Flowering,* 74, 86–87, no. 112, figs. 112a, 112b; Backhouse, "Tilliot Hours," 176–77, 180 n. 18; Backhouse, "The Tilliot Hours: Comparisons and Relationships," 213, 217–18, 223, fig. 8; Avril and Reynaud, *Manuscrits à peintures,* 307, 315, 317, 318 (twice), no. 174, illus.; Girault, "Jean Poyet," fig. 1.

Jean d'Auton, *Complainte sur la mort de dame Thomassine Espinolle*
Paris, Bibliothèque Nationale de France, MS fr. 1684
    Avril and Reynaud, *Manuscrits à peintures,* 314.

Jean d'Auton, *Complainte sur la mort de dame Thomassine Espinolle*
Paris, Bibliothèque Nationale de France, MS fr. 25419
    Avril and Reynaud, *Manuscrits à peintures,* 314.

Missal
Paris, Bibliothèque Nationale de France, MS lat. 850
    V. Leroquais, *Les sacramentaires et les missels manuscrits des bibliothèques publiques de France,* Paris, 1924, III, 216–17, no. 793, pls. C, CI; Plummer, *Last Flowering,* 87; Avril and Reynaud, *Manuscrits à peintures,* 317, 318.

Abbreviated Psalter
Paris, Bibliothèque Nationale de France, MS lat. 2844
    Avril and Reynaud, *Manuscrits à peintures,* 306–07, 314.

Secret des secrets and Alain Chartier, *Bréviaire des nobles*
Paris, Bibliothèque Nationale de France, MS n. a. fr. 18145
    Backhouse, "The Tilliot Hours: Comparisons and Relationships," 228; Avril and Reynaud, *Manuscrits à peintures,* 307, 313–14, no. 172, illus.

Single leaf of the Virgin and Child, from a Book of Hours
Paris, Musée du Louvre, Département des Arts Graphiques, R.F. 3890
    Plummer, *Last Flowering,* 87; Avril and Reynaud, *Manuscrits à peintures,* 317–18, no. 175, illus.

Single leaf of the Lamentation, from a Book of Hours
Philadelphia, Free Library, Rare Book Department, Lewis E M11:15a.
    C. U. Faye and W. H. Bond, *Supplement to the Census of Medieval and Renaissance Manuscripts in the United States and Canada,* New York, 1962, 459, no. XI:15.

Pierre Louis de Valtan, *Super qualibet dictione symboli apostolici*

Rotthalmünster, Antiquariat Heribert Tenschert

Backhouse, "Pierre Sala," 174 n. 21; Backhouse, "Tilliot Hours," 176; Backhouse, "The Tilliot Hours: Comparisons and Relationships," 215, 217, fig. 4; Rotthalmünster, Antiquariat Heribert Tenschert, *Leuchtendes Mittelalter II* (Katalog XXV), Rotthalmünster, 1990, 662–75, no. 57, illus.; Avril and Reynaud, *Manuscrits à peintures,* 307; Backhouse, "Poyet, Jean," 405.

Drawings

Coronation of King David
American private collection

Mocking of Elisha
Chicago, Art Institute, Department of Prints and Drawings, acc. no. 1965.16

Cain Killing Abel and *Sacrifice of Isaac*
London, British Museum, Department of Drawings (2 drawings), acc. nos. 1874-6-13-538 and 1874-6-13-539

Joseph Sold into Slavery
Rotterdam, Museum Boijmans Van Beuningen, inv. no. F.I.1

Bibliography for all drawings: Backhouse, "Tilliot Hours," 179; Backhouse, "The Tilliot Hours: Comparisons and Relationships," 224–27, figs. 12–15; Avril and Reynaud, *Manuscrits à peintures,* 308, 315, 318; Backhouse, "Poyet, Jean," 405; Burton L. Dunbar and Edward J. Olszewski, eds., *Drawings in Midwestern Collections: A Corpus Compiled by the Midwest Art History Society. Volume I: Early Works,* Columbia (Mo.), 1996, 120–26, no. 23; New York, Christie's, *Old Master Drawings,* sale catalogue, 10 January 1996, lot 176, illus.

Painting

Passion Triptych: *Christ Carrying the Cross, Crucifixion, and Entombment*

Loches, Château

Grete Ring, *A Century of French Painting, 1400–1500,* London, 1949, 216, no. 147, pl. 95; Plummer, *Last Flowering,* 87; Backhouse, "The Tilliot Hours: Comparisons and Relationships," 223; Claude Schaefer, *Jean Fouquet: An der Schwelle zur Renaissance,* Basel, 1994, 304–05, no. 5.9, illus.; Avril and Reynaud, *Manuscrits à peintures,* 306, 308, 309, 317, 318; Backhouse, "Poyet, Jean," 405.

SECTION B
BOOKS OF HOURS AND LITURGY

The two most accessible and useful works on Books of Hours are by Roger Wieck. Both were connected with major exhibitions, one at the Walters Art Gallery in Baltimore in 1988, the other at the Pierpont Morgan Library in New York in 1997: *Time Sanctified* and *Painted Prayers.* Since the latter publication updates the annotated bibliography of the former, there is little point in repeating either here. A Latin/English Book of Hours is now available on Dr. Glenn Gunhouse's Web site, "Hypertext Book of Hours" (address: http://members.tripod.com/~gunhouse/hourstxt /hrstoc.htm); the text is based on a Latin/English edition printed in Antwerp in 1599.

Among several handbooks containing information on liturgy, the following are particularly useful: *The Oxford Dictionary of the Christian Church,* F. L. Cross and E. A. Livingstone, eds., London, 1974; *The New Westminster Dictionary of Liturgy and Worship,* J. G. Davies, ed., Philadelphia, 1986; and various entries in *The Catholic Encyclopedia;* and in the *Dictionary of the Middle Ages,* Joseph R. Strayer, ed., 13 vols., New York, 1982–89.

In addition to the above, the following are good introductions to Christian feasts: K. A. Heinrich Kellner, *Heortology: A History of the Christian Festivals from their Origin to the Present Day,* London, 1908; Francis X. Weiser, *Handbook of Christian Feasts and Customs: The Year of the Lord in Liturgy and Folklore,* New York, 1952; Abbot

Guéranger, *The Liturgical Year,* 15 vols., Westminster, 1948–49.

Lancelot C. Sheppard's *Liturgical Books,* New York, 1962, is a good introduction to the subject. For more-detailed works on the Mass, see: Joseph A. Jungmann, *The Mass of the Roman Rite: Its Origins and Development (Missarum Sollemnia),* 2 vols., New York, 1950; and Adrian Fortescue and J. B. O'Connell, *The Ceremonies of the Roman Rite Described,* Westminster, 1958. Pierre Batiffol's *History of the Roman Breviary,* London, 1912, remains one of the best works on the subject. Andrew Hughes's *Medieval Manuscripts for Mass and Office: A Guide to their Organization and Terminology,* Toronto, 1982, offers very specific information regarding ceremony and a good bibliography.

SECTION C
SAINTS AND ICONOGRAPHY

The following books on saints are easily accessible: *The Catholic Encyclopedia,* although more thorough than most people need, is available at most public libraries. The same is true for *Butler's Lives of the Saints,* Herbert Thurston and Donald Attwater, eds., 4 vols., New York, 1963, which relates detailed information on the lives and cults of many major saints. F. G. Holweck's *Biographical Dictionary of the Saints,* St. Louis, 1924 (reprinted in Detroit, 1969), contains brief digests for an exhaustive collection of saints. The slender volume, *Dictionary of Christian Lore and Legend,* London, 1983, by J. C. J. Metford, contains interesting and obscure information. Jacobus de Voragine's *Golden Legend,* translated and adapted from the Latin by Granger Ryan and Helmut Ripperger, New York, 1969, was the medieval world's sourcebook on saints (it contains interpretations of saints' origins, legends, and miracles and is thus quite fundamental for understanding the medieval layperson's relationship with saints).

Easily accessible, but not comprehensive, is David Hugh Farmer, *The Oxford Dictionary of Saints,* Oxford, 1982. R. L. P. Milburn, *Saints and*

their Emblems in English Churches, London, 1949, also contains useful information relative to cults in England. Sean Kelly and Rosemary Rodgers, *Saints Preserve Us!* New York, 1993, is an irreverent and amusing digest of legends; it also has much information on saintly patronage.

Also useful are the following: *The Book of Saints: A Dictionary of Servants of God Canonised by the Catholic Church, Extracted from the Roman and Other Martyrologies,* compiled by the Benedictine Monks of St. Augustine's Abbey, Ramsgate, London, 1921; Helen Roeder, *Saints and their Attributes with a Guide to Localities and Patronage,* London, 1955; and Eliza Allen Starr, *Patron Saints,* 2 vols., Chicago, 1887.

The two most exhaustive collections of the lives of saints, however, are S. Baring-Gould's *Lives of the Saints,* 16 vols. (the last volume with a useful thematic index), Edinburgh, 1914, and Paul Guérin's *Les petits bollandistes: Vies des saints de l'Ancien et du Nouveau Testament . . . ,* 17 vols., Paris, 1880.

The two most common, and probably the most useful, books on basic Christian iconography and symbolism are George Ferguson, *Signs and Symbols in Christian Art,* London, 1954; and James Hall, *Dictionary of Subjects and Symbols in Art,* revised edition, New York, 1979. Volume 3 of Émile Mâle's *Religious Art in France,* entitled *The Late Middle Ages: A Study of Medieval Iconography and Its Sources,* Princeton, 1986, contains much about saints' images during the period of the creation of the Hours of Henry VIII. Herbert Friedmann's *Bestiary for Saint Jerome: Animal Symbolism in European Religious Art,* Washington, 1980, is especially useful in tracing the iconography of Jerome. Although the various volumes by George Kaftal focus on saints in Italian painting, they do give valuable source material: *Iconography of the Saints . . . ,* 4 vols., Florence, 1952–85.

The three best compendia of Christian iconography are the following: Louis Réau, *Iconographie de l'art chrétien,* 6 vols., Paris, 1955–59; Engelbert Kirschbaum, *Lexikon der christliche Ikonographie,* 8 vols., Freiburg, 1968; and Gertrud Schiller, *The*

Iconography of Christian Art, 2 vols., Greenwich (Conn.), 1971–72.

SECTION D
FULL-CITATION LIST

Avril, François, and Nicole Reynaud, *Les manuscrits à peintures en France, 1440–1520,* Paris, 1993.

Backhouse, Janet, "Pierre Sala, Emblesmes et devises d'amour," in *Renaissance Painting in Manuscripts: Treasures from the British Library,* Thomas Kren, ed., New York, 1983, 169–74.

————, "Poyet, Jean," in *The Dictionary of Art,* Jane Turner, ed., London, 1996, XXV, 405–06, illus.

————, "Tilliot Hours," in *Renaissance Painting in Manuscripts: Treasures from the British Library,* Thomas Kren, ed., New York, 1983, 175–80.

————, "The Tilliot Hours: Comparisons and Relationships," *British Library Journal,* XIII/2, 1987, 211–31.

The Catholic Encyclopedia, Charles G. Herbermann et al., eds., 16 vols., New York, 1910.

Copenhagen, Nationalmuseet, *Gyldne Bøger: Illuminerede middelalderlige håndskrifter i Danmark og Sverige,* Copenhagen, 1952.

Girault, Pierre-Gilles, "Jean Poyet peut-il être l'auteur des heures du Tilliot?" *Revue de l'art,* CX, 1995, 74–78.

Laborde, Léon Emmanuel Simon Joseph, marquis de, *La Renaissance des arts à la cour de France: Études sur le seizième siècle,* 2 vols., Paris, 1850–55.

Plummer, John, with the assistance of Gregory Clark, *The Last Flowering: French Painting in Manuscripts, 1420–1530, from American Collections,* New York, 1982.

Randall, Lilian M. C., assisted by Christopher Clarkson and Jeanne Krochalis, *Medieval and Renaissance Manuscripts in the Walters Art Gallery. Volume II: France 1420–1540,* Baltimore, 1992.

Wieck, Roger S., *Painted Prayers: The Book of Hours in Medieval and Renaissance Art,* New York, 1997.

Wieck, Roger S., with contributions by Lawrence R. Poos, Virginia Reinburg, and John Plummer, *Time Sanctified: The Book of Hours in Medieval Art and Life,* New York, 1988.

Wieck, Roger S., with a contribution by K. Michelle Hearne, *The Prayer Book of Anne de Bretagne: MS M.50, The Pierpont Morgan Library, New York,* Lucerne, 1999. This commentary, difficult to find, contains the discussion of Poyet's oeuvre that is repeated, with updating, in the present book.